AN AMERICAN HARVEST

An
AMERICAN
HARVEST

How One Family
Moved from Dirt-Poor Farming
to a Better Life in the Early 1900s

Cardy Raper

GREEN WRITERS PRESS *Brattleboro, Vermont*

Printed in the United States

10 9 8 7 6 5 4 3 2 1

Green Writers Press is a Vermont-based publisher whose mission
is to spread a message of hope and renewal through the words and
images we publish. Throughout we will adhere to our commitment to
preserving and protecting the natural resources of the earth. To that
end, a percentage of our proceeds will be donated to environmental
activist groups. Green Writers Press gratefully acknowledges support
from individual donors, friends, and readers to help support the
environment and our publishing initiative.

Giving Voice to Writers & Artists Who Will Make the World a Better Place
Green Writers Press | Brattleboro, Vermont
www.greenwriterspress.com

ISBN: 978-0-9962676-2-5

Visit the author's website at
www.cardyraper.com

PRINTED ON PAPER WITH PULP THAT COMES FROM FSC-CERTIFIED FORESTS, MANAGED FORESTS
THAT GUARANTEE RESPONSIBLE ENVIRONMENTAL, SOCIAL, AND ECONOMIC PRACTICES BY
LIGHTNING SOURCE ALL WOOD PRODUCT COMPONENTS USED IN BLACK & WHITE, STANDARD
COLOR, OR SELECT COLOR PAPERBACK BOOKS, UTILIZING EITHER CREAM OR WHITE BOOKBLOCK
PAPER, THAT ARE MANUFACTURED IN THE LAVERGNE, TENNESSEE PRODUCTION CENTER ARE
SUSTAINABLE FORESTRY INITIATIVE® (SFI®) CERTIFIED SOURCING

To the memory of my precious husband John,
the reddest of the redheads

CONTENTS

The Raper Homestead.

PROLOGUE

FRANK RAPER didn't feel too good. He'd survived a massive heart attack about a year earlier in 1910 and hadn't been much use since. His older boys helped out as much as they could: preparing beds for the Bright Leaf tobacco seeds to sprout their way to seedlings, plowing the fields in readiness for planting, tilling, topping, suckering as each plant put out unwanted shoots. Then followed harvesting and stringing the good leaves on poles over in the curing barn where Frank and the boys took turns stoking the fires night and day till each blade reached that perfect yellow gold.

The crop had gone to market. Frank rocked on the porch, savoring the lingering sweet smell of well-cured tobacco. He gathered strength as wife Julie lay in bed with early signs of labor bringing forth their eighth child. The older two, Cletus and Luther, had gone back to high school away in Churchland.

Frank called the rest together. "Arthur, Ralph, Howard, Blanche, Kenneth, you're all going to Uncle Dave's for the night. Arthur, you see to it your brothers and sister get there with pajamas and clean clothes for the morning."

Oh, I know what's coming, thought Arthur. They're going to call Doctor Bob with his little black bag, and when we get back home there'll be another squalling baby in that worn-out cradle.

Sure enough, the very next day, October 3, 1911, those five Raper children came home after breakfast to find a tiny baby boy sleeping peacefully beside their loving mother. This one had red hair like the last three, Kenneth, Blanche, and Howard. They called him John. In a few more years, he'd be another welcome farmhand in this rural North Carolina community called Welcome.

I married grown-up baby John in 1949. A distinguished scientist by the time I knew him, John's childhood haunted him still. The youngest of eight, he grew up tasting the red dust of that farm of his youth and its main cash crop: tobacco. Resentful memories of never-ending chores: hauling water, slopping pigs, milking cows, plowing fields, setting crops, suckering tobacco—row upon row in the blistering sun of summer—all took hold and stuck. It wasn't so bad when the brothers shared, but ultimately they left to seek more profitable livelihoods elsewhere. It was a time John could not forget. Yet John's ties to his brothers and sister stayed strong. All urban professionals, they nonetheless gathered in family reunion every five years and exchanged Round Robin letters in between.

In 1965, it was our turn to plan the reunion. After six-teen years of marriage and thirteen years of parenthood, I'd heard about this family from John's point of view. I wanted to learn more. Why did each and every one leave that hard-working God-fearing way of life, where discontented peers found mischievous and shocking diversions: steal-ing watermelons, bullying, mutilating, even murdering the vulnerable? Not one of John's siblings grew up to continue farming, like so many of their neighboring friends and rela-tives. From a one-room schoolhouse, they all sought higher education and professional accomplishments elsewhere—though their parents never went beyond seventh grade. How did that happen?

John and I booked an inn in Boothbay Harbor, Maine, because of its ocean breezes, its lobsters, clams, and pleas-ant dining spot facing an expansive lawn that sloped to a shimmering pond with a swimming dock and paddleboats.

Forty-eight members of the Raper family, all related in some fashion to long-dead William Franklin and Julia Crouse Raper, assembled the first week of August. All but one of John's siblings attended. Cletus, the oldest, had died since the last reunion.

I asked them to come prepared to talk about their time together as youngsters on the farm. John and I had just pur-chased a tape recorder to preserve their words.

After three days of romping about, chatting, swimming, boating, and feasting on fruits of the ocean, we settled down in one large room to hear what these brethren had to say.

This is the scene: It is evening. Children and spouses crowd on and about two king-sized beds facing a large rectangular table at one end of the room where the Raper siblings position themselves in the following order.

Arthur, third son, presides at head of table, and, by common assent, assumes the moderator's role. With shaggy grey hair, he sits erect looking every bit the part of a man in charge. As an official of the US State Department, Arthur had traveled the world—Japan, Iraq, Iran, Afghanistan, Pakistan—advising heads of government on matters of sociological and agricultural importance during the aftermath of World War II. Extensively published—author of seven scholarly books—he comes equipped with many writings and documents.

Ralph, fourth son, perhaps the handsomest, sits properly straight and tall. With neatly trimmed hair, light rimmed glasses, and half smile, he is the only brother wearing jacket and tie. A cotton economist with the US Department of Agriculture, Ralph comes bearing poems that set the scenes with vignettes of nostalgic childhood memories.

Luther, former director of membership relations for the Southern States Farmers' Cooperative, and eldest of the living lot, sets his younger siblings straight on some of their recollections. Of jovial temperament, he is mindful of differing feelings and tends to smile a lot.

Howard, middle child and first of the redheads, manifests an overseeing manner befitting his profession as president of a savings and loan company. Although the wealthiest family member, he displays a tendency of self-deprecation for not having done so well in school, especially when it came to spelling. Howard, like Luther, sits relaxed and smiles often.

Blanche, the second redhead and only female, appears determined yet demure. She teaches history and English in high school and has a penchant for writing poetry of philosophical and romantic bent, setting some to music. Blanche holds her own vis-à-vis all those brothers, refusing to suffer their guff.

Redheads **Kenneth** and **John** sit side-by-side and vie for attention as youngest of the lot. Both are distinguished university professors specializing in the science of fungi, and both are recipients of numerous accolades for their contributions to science.

Ken, the older, balding with red hair, claims fame as discoverer of the first strain of *Penicillium* capable of producing industrial amounts of the antibiotic penicillin during World War II. Tenured at the University of Wisconsin, he is author of four scholarly books.

John, fully redheaded, is professor of botany at Harvard University and a world-renowned expert on sexual reproduction in fungi.

Despite similar interests, Kenneth conveys an air of acceptance, smiling benignly most of the time, while John, not so benign, expresses resentment for having been put upon by all those older brothers.

Cletus, the oldest sibling, now gone, became the office manager of a large construction company and co-invented a balloon tire (for which he never won a patent). He had died of a heart attack since the previous family reunion and is fondly remembered here by all his brethren.

These siblings speak of life growing up on a dirt-poor farm with no modern conveniences but a plentitude of religious teachings and manual labor. They recount their hard-fought struggle to get an education and leave the farm for a more rewarding livelihood elsewhere. Their family reminiscences personalize a widespread movement from farm to urban ventures in early twentieth-century America.

Organized more or less by subject, the Rapers' readings are in italics; their discussions are in Roman and here is what this family has to say along with occasional musings of my own set off by italics and an ornament.

You are invited to listen.

ABOVE: Raper siblings at 1965 reunion: Howard, Ralph, Luther, Blanche, Kenneth, Arthur, and John.

RIGHT: Julia and Frank just married.

AN AMERICAN HARVEST

Julia and Frank with six of their offspring: daughter-in-law:
Rachel and Luther next to them; John, Howard, Kenneth,
Ralph, and Blanch, seated in front yard of homestead in 1927.

CHAPTER 1

Never be Idle

ARTHUR:
Now we shall think about things that happened long ago, when Momma and Papa were alive and we were children about the age of some of our own youngsters here. They will be interested to know what life was like when we were coming along at the ages they are now, and I think it will be satisfying for us to recall it. Some of us have written things down in preparation for this. Ralph, I know you have; let's start with you.

RALPH:
I have entitled this "I Remember." Although my main interests now are not generally associated with yesteryears, I shall respect Cardy's request and list a few of the impressions, experiences, conditions, and situations I still remember. The mere fact that another's memory may be different from mine doesn't mean that mine is wrong and his is right, or that his is right and mine is wrong. They may both be wrong.

I remember the house in which I was born
Located on the crest of a hill
Containing, first, four finished rooms and two porches,
Then another room finished
Still later another
Then two more rooms along with an upstairs porch.

I remember the old well in the yard
And the problems involved in keeping an adequate supply
    of water
Taking out the walls and digging it deeper on two occasions
And the unwelcome guests that occasionally fell in the water
Before the concrete floor was built around it.

I remember the persimmon trees in the cow pasture across the
    road from the house
Picking the persimmons up off the ground
And eating them without a thought of bugs, germs, filth,
    or radioactivity.

I remember pitching hay from small shocks in the meadow
Onto the wagon and, from it, onto stacks,
Going from one to five
Stopping for supper
And again, from six to eight, before calling it a day.

I remember stooping over
Moving up and down the rows
Setting out tobacco plants
hour after hour
And upon trying to stand erect,
finding it almost impossible.

JOHN:

Ralph, I'm still stooped over! Planting and suckering tobacco made a lasting impression on me. I would like to know how many of you feel as I do—that I was singled out for particular lone duty on hot afternoons in tobacco fields when everybody else was doing something less onerous. I have grown up, boy and man, feeling that I spent more unattended and unaccompanied hours in the smelly, dirty tobacco fields than any of the rest of you could have, and I want to know if there's any basis in fact for this; or was it just that I was particularly sensitive or lazy?

LUTHER:

I have known all these years you've felt this way, John, and there are some grounds for it. The primary difference is this: In the early years there were four or five of us in the tobacco field; when you carried the burden, all the rest of us were gone off to school. Papa wasn't able to be out with you, so you were all by yourself. And it is an uninteresting thing pulling worms and breaking suckers with nobody else to help.

"What's suckering?" asks one of the assembled.

LUTHER:

Suckering is pinching off the smaller unproductive leaves so the bigger healthier ones can grow better—you get more smoking leaves that way. It's a right sticky, messy job. You can make it a social affair if there are several of you, and a lot of talking did go on. I see it this way, John, and I know how you have felt.

JOHN:
I think one reason I've smoked so much is that I've been trying to get back at it.

HOWARD:
Papa didn't have anyone else to call on and nobody else to pass it on to.

JOHN:
You would know, Howard, being in the middle. But that's not the whole of it. Recall also, you chums knew our father when he was well and not so irritable. He had his massive heart attack before my birth. I never knew him as a strong, robust man. By the time I arrived, the hard labor on the farm was left mostly to those of the sons who were temporarily unable to find more diverting and less strenuous occupation elsewhere; and you all were better at finding that than I.

HOWARD:
We'd had more experience; we were older than you!

JOHN:
And still are—as you often care to remind me. I envy Ralph that he can recall the bucolic diversions with so much pleasure. These made less lasting impression on me than did the work, or perhaps worse, the ever-present threat of work.

❧ *As John's wife, I shared his vexation over dominating older siblings, for I too was born last in a large family of boisterous older brothers. Perhaps as the only girl, I felt the domination more than he, although in different ways. Our family had a farm. We didn't live on it—my father grew up there. Then, urged on by his much older brother, he left to become a small-town lawyer around 1907. By the time I came along, the farm still stood, run by my oldest brother, Paul. I and the other brothers helped out now and then. I thought it mostly fun, a break from city life and schooling. I pitched hay, picked apples, fetched water, tramped the silo, and ultimately felt proud to get promoted to driving the manure spreader all by myself. John found that kind of work no fun at all—just a burden.*

I think I didn't realize how deeply it affected him until I listened to his comments. ∾

LUTHER:

There was right much work, always something to do. I brought along a diary I'd kept for two to three years when I was in my teens. It'll give some idea of all the different kinds of work there was to do on the farm in those days. This was of course before I'd defected, as John put it—defected for good anyway.

I was getting my schooling down at Churchland then, so I wasn't around the better part of the winter months, but it seems like I made up for it come spring, summer, and fall; we didn't have many months of school in those days like the children do now.

Here are some entries right after school was out in April, 1915, a week after Easter:

> *Monday, 12. Cut a spoke tree* (an oak used primarily for wagon wheel spokes), *sawed and split posts and went to singing at Enterprise. Weather fair.*

> *Tuesday, 13. Hauled rails* (I spelled it 'halled'!), *dug post-holes, harrowed, and planted posts. Went to store at night. Weather clear.*

Thursday, 15. Planted corn, about 6 acres, and split spokes. Weather fair.

Thursday, 22. (You see, I skipped a day or so here and there—must have been too tired from working to write every day.) *Cut out cantaloupe ridges, Went to Giles Glen's funeral. Hauled manure and plowed. Weather fair.*

Wednesday, 28. Plowed by mill pond and hauled water, harrowed, cemented smokehouse floor. (I have that cemented spelled with an "s.") *Made a milk trough and went to Miz Ida Carver's at night to sing, Weather fair.*

(Then, just to give an idea of what August was like, I'll skip over.)

Monday, 16. Helped work the road towards Friedberg and worked Irish potatoes. Went to preaching at night. Weather fair. (You see, that time in August we were working right much with the tobacco crop, and we had to go to preaching too. That was part of the annual revival meeting. We all went and had to fit the work around it somehow.)

Thursday, 19. Suckered tobacco. Went to preaching, cleaned out tobacco barns. Weather fair.

Friday, 20. Cut with disk, sowed turnips at tobacco barn, sowed crimson clover in late corn. Suckered tobacco and gathered a load of melons. Weather threatening.

Monday, 23. Ploughed for wheat and went to preaching at night. Weather clear.

And so on it goes.

I'll reflect back on the importance of those spoke trees I mentioned. I was closer to it than the younger boys, for it was in our time that most of those oaks were cut for spokes. The younger generation folks can hardly appreciate this.

We may live too well today—a very different economic situation—but we would run out of money on the farm. I mean run out of money! There wouldn't be *any* money. And it would be the fall of the year, the tobacco not yet ready to sell, and eight children to buy shoes for. We bought some ready-made clothes, though Mother made most of our clothes in the early days.

We'd get down to the last penny, and Papa would decide whether we had a load of hay we could take to town. If any hay could be spared, we'd take it to town. If we didn't have hay, there was something else we could depend on and that was to cut a spoke-tree. We would go cut straight, smooth, white oak trees into blocks a little longer than wagon spokes, and split them up into hunks of wood, two inches by three inches.

Out of each of these, the Nissen Wagon Company at Waughtown would make spokes for wagons and carriages and such. Papa would take me one time with him when he went to sell the spokes, take Arthur the next trip, and Ralph the next. That was one of the few ways we got our social life, going to the city. Each load would give us a few dollars. Fifteen or twenty dollars would buy enough pairs of two-dollar shoes, and that's how really close we ran sometimes.

How our parents kept their composure as well as they did under those conditions is more than I can now understand. At the time it seemed to be normal, for everyone was doing more or less the same thing.

Homestead and barns on eroded turf.

The horse barn outlived all the others.

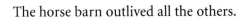

Grandchild, Billy, learns one of the chores.

Tending the curing
shed fire. PHOTO ARCHIVES

Tending the tobacco crop. PHOTO ARCHIVES

Curing the leaves. PHOTO ARCHIVES

CHAPTER 2

Be Always Learning

RALPH:

I remember money was always scarce at our house,
So my brother and I decided we would show Papa he could
*   save lots of money*
By not putting any fertilizer under the tobacco.
In making up the ridges
We skipped one row and gave the row next to it a double
*   serving.*
When the tobacco in the field was ready to top, about thirty
*   inches high*
The tobacco in the "convincing" row was only a foot high
But in the double row, had by then been topped.
   You remember this, Arthur?

ARTHUR:

I do, and this is what I have on that.

   Every spring, I remember from early childhood, there

was the strain of getting enough cash to buy commercial fertilizer, particularly for the tobacco. This seemed to me a very hard condition to meet. The truth is I didn't believe the fertilizer was so badly needed, but Dad did.

So, each late winter or early spring, he went to the woods and chopped down a virgin white oak tree or two and sawed and split them into size for wagon spokes (Luther made mention of that). I'll never forget how hard and how cold these spokes were as we hauled them, often leaving home before daybreak, to the Nissen Wagon Works at Waughtown, a couple miles southeast of Winston-Salem. It took two or three day's work in the woods to get a load of spokes ready, and then another full day to take them to Waughtown.

Well, the point is, as I said, I didn't really think that the fertilizer was that important, and then at about eight years of age and having the conviction of my doubts, I decided to prove the situation.

The opportunity came late one evening just before dark in the lower part of the field where the schoolhouse now stands. I was putting fertilizer into the open tobacco rows by hand from a bucket; Luther or Ralph, I forget who, was ridging a couple of rows behind me. I put a double dose of fertilizer in one row, and left the next without any. Since it was nearly dark, the ridging was completed with nobody but me knowing about the experiment.

When the tobacco plants began to grow I, naturally, watched to see what would happen. Every day or so I would go by and look, and shortly it was perfectly clear to me that the plants on the doubly fertilized row were looking fine, and the plants on the other were small and irregular in size—in fact, puny. Well, a week or ten days *later, at the dinner table one evening, Dad said, "You know, something happened out there in the lower part of that tobacco patch. It looks to me like somebody put double fertilizer on one row and skipped the next."*

Well, that was that. I too found out we did need fertilizer, and this became all the clearer by the time the tobacco was ready to harvest, for then, the doubly fertilized row, having matured early and evenly, was the best tobacco I had seen on our farm. As a matter of fact, the next year, I could have been sold on putting double fertilizer under every row.

Now here, see how differently this is recalled. It is essentially the same story as Ralph's, but the details have become changed over the years, with some of them having wobbled off here and there.

BLANCHE:
I remember hearing about those tobacco rows, but this is the first time I ever knew it was done deliberately.

LUTHER:
Well, I have another kind of fertilizer story. As I grew up, and you boys will remember, I accumulated quite a library of US Agricultural Bulletins; in fact, I had 2,100 of them at one time. I had them indexed, and double indexed. In those days, we had what we called Farmers' Institutes, and, at that time, super phosphate was called "acid." At these Farmers' Institutes we heard a lot about acid soils to grow clover and crops and what have you.

My face still gets red when I think about it, but I had quite an argument with Papa once, that he shouldn't be putting the acid on the soil, because it needed lime instead of acid. Well, it turned out later, the name "acid" was changed to super phosphate, and it was an essential and important plant food.

He was right all the time. I never apologized—yet I did know better before he died, for I had gone to college and studied some of these things, so knew something about it. But I was so ashamed that I never did make mention to him that I was mistaken. I've been sorry ever since for being such a smart aleck. I was at an Agricultural College, and I graduated from that thing with reasonably good grades—I guess I thought I ought to know—but I was dead wrong, and Papa was right.

ARTHUR:
I recollect a time along in there when you were right and dad was wrong—out of sheer orneriness. You sent home a new scientific formula for feeding a pig. Kenneth was to be the fellow to perform this particular experiment.

KENNETH:
That's how I earned my first ten dollars.

ARTHUR:
That's right. Well, Kenneth fed the pig out and it weighed very much heavier than any other pig in the whole country-side for the length of time that it had been fed. Considering the cost of the feed, it was perfectly clear that here was a better way to feed a pig. Dad, having three or four of us smart alecks in college by then, must have gotten tired of us trying to show him the way. I expect he must have thought to himself, *I've adjusted to as much of this as I'm going to;*

I'm going to hold on to something myself. Well, at any rate, he took a position, and just disposed of it with one decisive statement: "That's no way to feed a pig." And so, we didn't feed any more pigs that way.

KENNETH:
Our father was right on the button though when it came to insurance. None of us would have called it so well. He took out insurance one year for damage by hail to the tobacco crop. For the first time in all the years of growing tobacco we got one huge hailstorm. It riddled the crop and Father collected for damages. He never bought hail insurance again—and we never had any more damaging hailstorms.

BLANCHE:
Why, Papa just cried when he lost that crop to the hail. I remember him standing there by the window looking out on it, and I remember the tears streaming down the sides of his face on into his big bushy mustache. I don't believe he had any insurance; leastwise I didn't know he did. I just felt so sorry for him, I went to my room and wrote a poem about it.

I don't have it—I didn't keep it—but I remember something of what was in it. I imagined him talking to Mama about the cash the tobacco was going to bring in— he called her Sally in the poem—and how it would have been enough to pay off the second mortgage on the farm and to keep the boys in college. Then he went on to explain a lot of things about what he thought was important in life: working together with others for the better of the community, educating people, and all those attitudes that made him a special person.

JOHN:
You're an incurable romantic, Blanche. In the first place, the tobacco crop couldn't even be seen from any window in our house. In the second place, Kenneth was right: Father did have the crop insured that year, and I don't remember any other time we had hail. 'Course there could have been an earlier hailstorm, before I was born.

BLANCHE:
Well, I think you're both wrong.

HOWARD:
Sister Blanche, come on and admit it; you know you're given to fancy.

ARTHUR:
This one I don't believe I can help settle out, for I wasn't there at the time. We must have weathered it all right.

KENNETH:
Oh, Arthur!

ARTHUR:
What I mean is I don't recall anyone having to be taken out of college at that time. In any case, tobacco farming was a risky business. Let me read something I have here, a bit of sociological commentary relating to just what you've been talking about. It's nothing profound, just a little something I brought along in case it seemed appropriate.

KENNETH:
Seems to me you brought a lot of "little somethings" along,

and my guess is they'll all seem appropriate before the evening's out.

ARTHUR:
Well, brother Kenneth, you might have done likewise; then we could be listening to yours.

KENNETH:
I didn't realize this session was going to turn into such a documentary.

ARTHUR:
We don't have many opportunities to go on together about some of these things. I believe we should take advantage of it while we've a mind to.

❧ *As Arthur says this, I'm thinking he reminds me of my middle brother Luther who,* <u>*born*</u> *'The Professor,' did a lot of pontificating, even as a child—he just knew too much and had to let it out. Brother Jonny (the youngest) and I figured Lute bested us in IQ scoring because, when asked to name all the nouns he could think of within a minute's time, he rattled off a memorized list of all the US state capitals.*

Then, when Lute actually became a bona fide university professor, he plied us with annual treatises on serious topics, like governmental development of newly planned towns. Despite his know-it-all bearing, I loved him dearly, and, incidentally, learned a lot. ❧

ARTHUR:
I'll just get on with what I've written about neighborly practices and how we shared.

When hail insurance could be had, first from a private insurance company and later as a public service, most farmers in our community took advantage of it. A farmer who did not insure his tobacco crop was soon looked upon as not deserving of neighborly assistance when hail did strike. In short, a man was expected to do what he could for himself and after that should come neighbors' help. Earlier, a hail storm that damaged the crop was looked upon as a warning from the Almighty that the victim hadn't been living right . . . providence, if you will.

But the folks in the community did help each other frequently. Mutual aid was a common practice when a man's barn burned down or when he and his family were sick and couldn't plant or harvest their crop. Our mother, especially, believed that anybody who was in trouble needed to be pitied and helped, rather than censured. Her notion was borne out when, upon the death of a local ne'er-do-well, the doctor stated he had been suffering from a weakening ailment for more than a decade.

Essentially, insurance—before people could buy it—was in the responsibility the folks felt for each other. In fact, a major part of our group activities was the informal swap-work arrangements among neighboring families. Besides barn-raising and crop-planting or harvesting, under unusual circumstances of fire or illness, we got together for hog-killings, corn-shuckings, and wood-choppings.

Hogs were killed on cold mornings, usually two or three families pooling their labor. A dish of "haslets," a stew of viscera—lungs, heart, liver, kidney, and pancreas—was served piping hot at the noon meal on the day of the killing. Later, liver-pudding and souse—a gelatinous head-cheese fixed from various parts of the hog's head and feet—were made.

Then, the women and children prepared sausage by squeezing the contents from the long casing of the small intestines, scraping off the musculature, attaching the casing to the spout of a grinder, and filling it with ground scraps of lean meat, some fat, sage, salt, and black and red pepper. The sausage was tied off at appropriate intervals and hung in the smokehouse to cure and dry for a couple of weeks. It would keep a couple of months.

The women also cleaned the large intestines and soaked them in vinegar to make chitlins, which appeared as a milky-white flaccid hose, looped back and forth upon itself and tied with a string. These were sold at the market. We didn't eat them, and I don't believe many other white families did either. Fried crisp in fat and properly seasoned, they were a favorite dish in Negro households.

The men did the butchering. Some fresh meat—chops and roasts—was saved for immediate consumption as were the hocks, feet, and ears. I have fond memories of the special crunchiness of boiled up pig ears. Hams, shoulders, and side meat were salted down for a time, then cured by hanging in a tight smokehouse over a smoldering hickory fire. These would last for many months.

❧ My John tried in vain to have our children and me cherish pig ears and feet. I went along for a bit—he did the cooking, boiling them up with a bit of celery, onion, salt and pepper—but the kids rebelled. John couldn't win. As with calf brains for breakfast, even he agreed, brain preparation involved just too much sliminess first thing in the morning. ❧

ARTHUR (*continues reading*):

Wood-choppings were scheduled when a family had cleared some woods to make a field. The trees were most likely felled during the winter months when there wasn't so much else to do. The neighborhood group assembled on some agreed-upon day to cut up the logs for fuel. Much wood was needed not only for heating the homes but also for firing the tobacco barns.

Our house was particularly drafty, and on a cold, blowy day a roaring wood fire in the fireplace did not keep us warm; it only helped. During the curing process those fires in the furnaces of the tobacco barns had to be fed day and night so as to maintain just the right temperature: 100 degrees Fahrenheit for two days then slowly increased over four or five days to 210 degrees. We'd take turns tending—maybe cook up some sweet potatoes, roastin' ears, or chestnuts to induce wakefulness during the long dark hours.

Communal pie supper.

Corn-shuckings happened in the evening. The men, boys, and girls stripped the husks from a mountain of ears while the women might sew on a quilt together and then serve up a luscious pie supper for all to enjoy once the work was done. These were especially sociable occasions, for there'd be a chance to chat and joke whil'st the work was getting accomplished.

RALPH:

Those pie suppers made all the work seem worthwhile—except over at Julius Jager's. He'd have us over to a corn-shucking, slaving away, and he'd never come out to work himself. He'd have his hired man pitch in, but we'd never even see Jager. The women didn't take to his place too kindly, so the food, if any at all, was inferior also. That man never even went to his neighbors' corn-shuckings. He didn't know the meaning of the word *exchange.*

KENNETH:

I don't remember him. Did anyone bother to go a second time to his corn shucking?

ARTHUR:

Oh, I guess we went two or three times before we smartened up. He'd send out his hired hand to other shuckings, but Ralph is right, he didn't go himself. He lost out in the end, I reckon.

There is one particular corn-shucking event that has stayed with me over the years:

It was at Thanksgiving time. Luther, Cletus, and I were home on vacation from high school—we were the only three boys, I guess, in the community who went away to school at that time. We went with Dad and the younger boys to a corn-shucking down at Henry Perryman's.

Along with everyone else there, we shucked corn and carried shucks into the barn and put them away in the mow for cow feed. Toward midnight, as we were carrying shucks into the barn, three of us boys—and I am not sure but that I was the leader—decided to pull a prank by pouring water on the other boys who were carrying shucks. The roof on the barn had holes in it, and maybe it was when we looked up through the roof and saw the stars that this nasty little idea came into our heads, or my head.

Well, at any rate, we went down to the well, pumped two buckets of water, and the three of us scrambled to the top of the barn with them. Now, this night would be the first frost of the year; it came late that year. When the other boys came in with their shucks, we waited until they got directly under us, and then we doused them. They didn't have any change of clothes there, and they near froze.

The parents did the natural thing; they very quickly asked one another, "Where were your boys?" We knew we were going to get caught—I think that encouraged me to confess a bit earlier than I normally would. It was a crazy thing to have done, just back from high school, in a sort of privileged position, and doing a fool thing like that.

I shall never forget seeing our dad stand there quietly taking the abuse, particularly from one man whose crippled son was wetted. The man cried, "Now you think you're doing something by sending your boys away to school; now what are you getting out of it?"

We knew we were wrong, double-dyed wrong, and said so, but Dad didn't ever lecture us on it. He didn't ever say anything to us. If he had just said something it would have eased it up a little.

HOWARD:

There were times, every few Sundays or so, when we would be invited out to our neighbors for dinner. It was quite fashionable, a general practice in fact. We would go down to Mr. Lindsay Zimmerman's, or over to Uncle Dave's, or up to Mr. Wilson's, or over to Mr. Tesh's. I recall quite well—when we would be invited down to Mr. Lindsay Zimmerman's— that quite frequently Miss Battie would leave church with us, and we would all go down there about twelve thirty or one o'clock.

Then they would go out and catch the chicken, kill it, pick it, and when they got it cooked, we'd have dinner. It became quite an affair, and in the meantime others were getting vegetables together—the whole meal fixed after we had left the church. This wasn't true in all places, but was in this particular case. Most families had made necessary preparations beforehand, and we didn't have to wait over an hour for lunch.

ARTHUR:

Except for the children and some of the women, maybe, who'd have to wait and eat at the second table.

HOWARD:

Yes, or even a third table sometimes.

BLANCHE:

I think we ought to make this remark about Miz Battie's dinner though. When you finally sat down to eat, you never sat down to a better meal.

LUTHER:
Except on one occasion, when I was a small boy—I was so embarrassed—she served some little cakes, and the ants were crawling all over them. I wasn't old enough to know better, so I said, "Miz Battie, there are ants in your cakes." I'll never forget it.

BLANCHE:
Naturally the ants liked her cakes; everybody did. Her spice and marble cakes were otherworldly, and her pies, oh my: blackberry, peach, dewberry, cherry. I could always make room for a piece even after eating all I thought I could hold of her stewed up chicken, biscuits and gravy, tasty thin slices of fried country ham, cukes and onions swimming in vinegar, buttered corn, lima beans, rape, mustard or turnip greens flavored with a bit of fat-back, or, as a special treat maybe, winter-cress, and a dollop of sweet potato with more milk gravy—there was always plenty of gravy.

My hunger was extra at Aunt Battie's house. Perhaps it was partly because there were three to four women present who'd do most of the fixin's, and I could be free to go play with the boys a bit before it was time for us little ones to eat. Food fixin' was all women's work and I was glad to be excused from it on such occasions.

I do now enjoy cooking, but that plus all the other things the women had to do made for a right physical type existence, the likes of which I'm glad I grew away from.

Of course if the Sunday dinner was at home I wouldn't be excused. Momma'd take charge, and I'd have to help all the way through the first, second, sometimes third servings. First we'd serve the men and any women who were part of a guest couple, then, if necessary, another table-full. The third finally would be mostly children, and Momma and I'd get to sit down for a spell.

   When I was a child, our Sunday dinners were special as well, but with almost all store-bought fixings. Out-of-season vegetables like peas and string beans came frozen by Mr. Birdseye, and the chicken would not have been running about an hour before cooking.

In warmer seasons, Mom sometimes packed a big picnic dinner; we'd invite friends and relatives and drive down to a big open place called Flat Rock surrounded by woods on our farm. We hunted for wild flowers, acorns, butternuts; dipped in the pool of a bordering stream, then warmed by the outdoor fireplace where fumes from grilling hamburgers, hotdogs, and store-bought buns whetted our appetites. We roasted marshmallows and crunched them between two Nabisco graham crackers laced with melting Hershey's chocolate bars for dessert.

Occasionally, when Pop came home with a wallet full of cash for some case he'd taken on, we'd drive to Montreal for a grand dinner out at the Queens Hotel where frugal Mom cautioned, "Read the menu from the less expensive meals at bottom, not the other way round."

As the only girl, I don't remember being called upon to put out a lot of effort in meal preparations. I helped, but not in the way of Blanche. I and my youngest brother, Jonny, occasionally earned spending money by helping out at Mom's formal dinner parties: I waitressed; Jonny washed dishes; I dried.

CHAPTER 3

Strive to Please

BLANCHE:
Like some of the rest of you, I wrote down some of my
memories before we met here tonight, and I'd like to read
the part describing our daily routine, mine, I mean, with
Momma.

We worked together a lot, Momma and I. We would
rise before dawn, and while the boys were out doing the
chores, we would start a good fire in the old wood stove.
As the kitchen slowly warmed, we prepared the breakfast.
It might be fried thin sliced ham or sausage with water
gravy and hot baking powder biscuits, or eggs and fried
mush. (Mush is corn meal boiled up the day before with
a little bacon, put aside to cool and glutinize, then sliced
and fried in bacon grease.) *Or we would fix a kind of*
cereal dish made up of crisp toasted homemade bread,
ground up and dowsed with sugar and cream. Then there
was pie: apple, peach, persimmon, pumpkin, or the old
standby sweet potato pie. Breakfast was big at our house.

HOWARD:
And mighty good after an hour or two's hard labor outside.

BLANCHE:
Sometimes I wished I could have traded places with you boys.

KENNETH:
Well, Blanche, we helped around the house some. I mean there were too many of us boys to leave all the housework to just you and Momma. Most other homes had a number of girls, and boys generally didn't help out much around the house, but our case was different. We always made our own beds; we often shared in setting the table, cleaning the house, clearing and washing the dishes.

HOWARD:
And carrying in the wood, the water, and taking out the slop. We had no plumbing of course, not even a kitchen sink with a drain. Had to go out to the well, lower the bucket about sixty feet to water level, raise it up full by cranking away on the windlass, then carry it into the house.

BLANCHE:
It's true, you boys did help some, and Momma never worked in the fields. I'd help a little at harvest time. Momma'd sometimes get the vegetables from the garden, but unlike other women in the community, she never cultivated the gardens around the house, and neither of us milked the cows.

In addition to the regular help from you boys, Arthur actually took over the housework for spells when Momma began having severe sick headaches before I was old enough to take charge. He did the cooking and ironing and directed the activities of us younger children. He was a good cook, and we bragged about him to the whole neighborhood.

ARTHUR:
That part, the bragging in the neighborhood, I particularly did not like.

BLANCHE:
Well, let me continue here with what I've written about my recollection of the daily chores.

After breakfast, nine in the mornings, we baked pies or bread and cooked for the men and boys who would come in at noon ravishingly hungry. Dinner was mostly vegetables of various kinds. That was during the long summer months; the rest of the year, when we children were going to school, we'd take a packed lunch.

In the afternoons we sewed, mended, or cut carpet rags. There was something akin to miraculous about taking old faded, ragged garments, cutting them into strips, tacking the ends of the strips together, winding the long strips into balls, then taking huge boxes of balls to the neighborhood weaver; and, a few weeks later, bringing home bright new carpeting to be the pride of the house.

Making shirts and dresses also brought satisfaction and wonderment at Momma's skill in copying pictured garments from mail-order catalogues such as Bellas-Hess and Montgomery Ward. A sewing machine ordered from Bellas-Hess made sewing easier. Nearly all of our clothes were hand made.

There was seasonal work also. We canned large quantities of vegetables and fruits at harvest time. A variety of beans, including black-eyed peas, were dried and stored. Beets, little and big cucumbers, got pickled and put away in jars. Sauerkraut, made by shredding cabbage, salting and packing it into an earthen crock, covering it with water and weighting it down with a rock on top of a china plate just big enough to fit into the top of the crock, was ready to eat after souring in its own juices for two to three weeks.

Potatoes, turnips, squash, when kept in the basement, lasted through the winter into spring. Hominy, a favorite at our table, was made by soaking dried corn kernels in lye and, after thorough rinsing, scrubbing the kernels between the hands to remove the softened seed coats. When boiled with a bit of fat-back it made a tasty dish.

All of these foods along with chickens and eggs, milk, cottage cheese, and butter—which we churned once a week—an occasional slaughtered calf and two or three hogs, kept us amply supplied throughout the year, We bought very little: only sugar, salt, and a few other condiments. Even our flour came from our wheat, which was ground at the local mill at Enterprise.

We never ate out at a restaurant. I didn't know what one looked like until I was grown. Besides Sunday dinner now and then at the home of relatives or friends, there was an occasional church supper, which we children were allowed to attend. These were our only opportunities to eat outside the home.

Of course this meant that Momma never, except in times of illness, obtained relief from kitchenly duties. The kitchen might change, the amount and kind of work might vary, but the need to prepare food never left.

And I can assure you boys that the work seemed, at times, as tedious to us womenfolk as the work in the fields must have seemed to you.

ARTHUR:

That may be, sister, it's the relentless pressure of such work that tends to get you down. To tell you the truth, I kind of enjoyed the times when I was brought in from the fields to work in the kitchen when Mother was feeling poorly, because it meant a change of scene for me. I protested some, naturally enough—I thought it not quite manly. But if that kind of nonsense hadn't prevailed (the notion that kitchen work was woman's work and fieldwork was man's work) I believe we might've switched off duties now and again just to relieve the tedium. It might have helped a good deal.

HOWARD:

Well, I may be old-fashioned, but I still think kitchen work is woman's work. I'll get on out there and push the mower over the grass, trim up the hedges, and such things like that, but I'll leave Miz Cat get on in there and fix the meals. She doesn't want me messin' around in her kitchen anyways.

ARTHUR:

As Blanch mentioned, our mother had sicknesses. She needed extra help, especially at those times when she was feeling poorly.

I want to read something I have about that:
I remember with great grief still her intense headaches, migraine, Dr. Bob called it. On one occasion she was sitting out on the back doorstep—said her head was about to burst. She said, "Go call Dad." I did, and he soon came.

She said, "Frank, if you will press my head from front to back just as hard as you can, I believe it will help." Dad was then quite a strong man, and I saw him hesitate, but when she again asked him to do it, he did. He took her head in his hands, front to back, and pressed firmly. She said, "No, that's not enough. If you can press much harder maybe it will help." He did. It seemed to me that her skull would crush under the force. It didn't. Her headaches continued.

BLANCHE:

Those headaches did continue, but between times she sang while she worked. She always sang. She sang hymns unless she wasn't feeling well; her silence was how we could tell when another sick spell was coming on.

HOWARD:

You know, Blanche, you failed to make mention of the special foods we had at Eastertime and Christmas. They were somewhat uplifting, you might say—the Moravian sugar cakes and colored eggs at Easter for example.

ARTHUR:

Those eggs tasted nearly as good as they looked, after the Easter Sunrise Service. Playing in the band at a cemetery that early in the morning cost a lot of wind and caused a mighty hunger. But the Service was always memorable— the beauty of the dawn coming on over the setting of row upon row of stretched out tombstones, reposing on the spring-green lawn patterned with long moving shadows of towering pines and oaks; and the sound of the brasses out

Moravian graveyard.

there in the openness, playing the grand old German cho-
rales—it always made me tearful almost.

It seemed a fitting way to celebrate Easter, and it's
one of the loveliest religious ceremonies anywhere. I've
missed it to this day since we left our childhood years in
Welcome.

Well then, there was Christmas too with its special tradi-
tions of the paper thin, spicy Moravian cookies, some can-
dies maybe, and oranges, and always the fun of choosing
and cutting just the right cedar for a tree to bring into the
house and trim up with popcorn, tinsel, and candles.

KENNETH:
Juniper.

ARTHUR:
How's that? Oh, the tree you're talking about. We always called them cedars.

JOHN:
That doesn't make them cedars.

ARTHUR:
Guess you're right at that. All right. We defer to you botanist boys. We trimmed a juniper tree for Christmas, which we in our ignorance called a cedar.

LUTHER:
Better change my ways, I reckon. I'm ignorant too, Arthur. I always called them cedars; do to this day.

But there were other special occasions: don't forget the ice-cream socials in the summertime—lawn parties we sometimes called them. Ice cream's never since tasted so good, made up of thick cream, eggs and sugar, with peaches, strawberries, bananas, or just plain vanilla or chocolate for flavoring. I'd take turns churning, and by the time it was ready, we were more than ready. My mouth readies now just thinking about it.

Then we young folks would sometimes play games at the socials or at the church suppers—you know, boy and girl games like Bingo-go-go where the girls tapped the boys they liked on the shoulder, or Farmer in the Dell, things like that. Perfectly innocent 'til a couple might sneak away from the crowd, out behind a barn or some trees and not be missed for a spell. I 'spect many a romance got started that way.

BLANCHE:
I know of some for sure. Then there was always blackberrying on the Fourth of July. Come storm or sun, we'd go en mass to pick blackberries all morning long—I usually ate more than I saved. To this day, I associate the Fourth of July with a queasy stomach and itchyness from chigger bites.

JOHN:
Those chiggers had a special affinity for the ankles, the middle, and certain private parts. They'd bother a guy something awful for weeks.

HOWARD:
Worse than the seven-year itch, 'cause there wasn't a thing a fellow could do about 'em except scratch.

There were no fireworks then, that place, that time. As a city girl in the nineteen thirties, I celebrated the birth of our nation by making noise and blowing up tin cans. Dad gave a dollar to each if us little kids to spend as we wished for punk, cherry bombs, fire crackers, snakes, salutes—all to perpetrate mayhem. Come evening, we packed a picnic and joined relatives up in the mountains to shoot off rockets, flares, pinwheels; watch the embers drift to the pond, sizzle, then snuff out—no chiggers, just an occasional itch from mosquito or black fly bites.

BLANCHE:

Well, after the blackberrying, besides scratching to do, there'd be blackberries to preserve—always plenty of work in the kitchen.

ARTHUR:

Yes, we worked hard on the farm. But then, we had Sundays, a day of rest from farming. Let's talk about how that felt.

CHAPTER 4

Beware of Evil

RALPH:

I remember Sundays being rather free from work
Except the daily chores
Going to Sunday School and staying for preaching, if any
Some mornings at Friedburg, four miles from home where
*   we were members*
But more often at Mount Olivet, up the road a quarter of a
*   mile*
Then again to Sunday School in the afternoon at Enterprise
A mile and a half away.

JOHN:

Most of our social activities were associated with three churches: the Moravian at Friedburg and Enterprise, and the Methodist, Mount Olivet. We attended them all—sometimes all three on the same Sunday. I think our parents were essentially Fundamentalists. I have something I've written about our parents' religious attitudes:

Friedberg Moravian church.

Mount Olivet Methodist church when the Rapers attended.

Young Blanche.

I remember, our home was bone dry, alcohol being held, along with card playing and dancing, as an instrument of the Devil, for the moral and spiritual corruption of the young and weak. I recall the harrowing chant of an itinerant preacher at one of those Revival meetings Luther mentioned: "Any man who can take a woman in his arms and go through the contortions of a modern dance without committing adultery in his heart is either more than a man, less than a man, or a damn liar." And our parents said, "Amen."

BLANCHE:
I reckon our mother believed that all right: I can't forget, when I left home for school, Mama tried to get me to promise I would not dance. I refused to promise—but I never had the heart to try.

Then, during vacations, the boys went on camping trips into the mountains with a party—including girls. I wasn't allowed to go. These were things I couldn't understand.

But I would take issue with John's saying our father was Fundamentalist. As a very little girl, I remember mentioning to him that a lot of people seemed to understand things about religion that I did not understand. Papa explained there were a lot of things he didn't understand either, but we did what we could. Religion, he said, was simply to help you to be good, and if people were good, this was what was important. You need not worry because you could not understand all of it.

I think Papa's idea was to broaden religion and to work more with other people. He seemed to want us to see there was no real difference between Methodists and Moravians and Baptists; I think it was more for this reason than for his Fundamentalism that we went to other churches and to so many of them.

JOHN:
I think perhaps you're idealizing his restlessness a bit.

KENNETH:
You know, John, you seem to be real bothered by this. I never thought much about it, I mean, the churches. They were there and we went to them, and we enjoyed the people who went to them. I never felt I was either free or hemmed in; this was just the way life was.

RALPH:
I agree largely with Blanche, I don't think our father was Fundamentalist at all. I think he was a character quite

different from most people in our community. He didn't run the farm too well, but he continually looked forward to better education, better roads, and things of that sort.

If I was surprised at anything as a child it was at the times when I *didn't* get scolded for something I thought a Fundamentalist would scold me for. He didn't make out that we'd go to Hell or the "booger man" would get us if we didn't do right by his sights.

ARTHUR:

You know, speaking of Fundamentalism, those Revival meetings Luther mentioned in his diary tried to instill such doctrines. I brought something I'd written long ago concerning my impressions of a particular revival meeting I attended when I was about fourteen. I wrote it some years after that, when I was at the University, in fact, but the recollection seemed fresh in my mind at the time.

REVIVAL MEETING

It was on a very warm day in August that I saw the buggies and carriages and pedestrians of the community gathering to the church. Those God-fearing men left their growing crops and growing grass to the care of no one; those women who rear children and bake pies and bread and cook beans also left their work undone, and all went to the church.

The regular minister of the church had a visiting minister to conduct the services. The regular minister would lead all the opening parts of the services. The visiting minister would sit behind the pulpit until time for him to deliver the sermon. This was the procedure of these meetings. When the meeting was about to end there was generally a proposition made. I did then hate those propositions. I couldn't understand them, and I was compelled through circumstances to respond to the proposition. (A proposition is a call to the altar to make a commitment to Christ.)

These meetings were held at ten o'clock and again at the eight o'clock, evening hour. The day meeting was chiefly for the saved; the night service was for those who were unsaved in the community. The meetings had begun on Sunday; no propositions were made at the earlier meetings; I enjoyed them very much.

The Monday morning meeting was a kind of preparatory meeting. The regular preacher told of the blessings the people, as Christians, should enjoy and also the convictions that the unsaved in the community should experience. With such preliminary remarks and a few hymns and a very long and earnest prayer offered by a very old and sincere man, the visiting minister opened the Bible and began to read from that blessed book.

He read very much, and there was some connection between the passages read. He exhorted the people to get on the Lord's side. He told of God's great plan of salvation. He showed in what way man was evil and condemned except through the death of Christ upon a cruel, heavy, hilltop-planted cross; how God's plan of salvation must be met if people are really glad and happy in Christ. After showing that man was condemned and had to be redeemed by Christ, he beckoned all those who wanted a real revival in the community to stand up. Everybody stood up.

I stood up. I really wanted to have a revival. I felt

that I needed aid. I felt that I was weak. I honestly meant what I said when I stood up. I wanted all people to be revived, me along with the group. Service was over at 12:45 P.M., and very soon each father and mother and child was making way towards a pot of well-cooked beans and roasting ears of corn.

The community had been blessed by that meeting. I felt good as I went down the hill by the tobacco barns and reached home, still thinking of that fine sermon and the noble desires expressed by all the folks there—an entire community desiring the same thing. Well surely a revival must come.

The people, by milking and feeding a little earlier than commonly, were assembled at the night service. The regular preacher took but very little part that night. The visiting minister took charge of the songs. He prayed a prayer of fineness. He asked God to open the hearts of any and all unsaved who might be there. He prayed that they might see the true light and turn and line as God would have them line. I enjoyed that prayer. It did me good. I never have said "Amen" in a service, but I did feel "Amen" all over.

The sermon was fine. He explained how God has a purpose for each of us to fill when he created us. We were all created for some service to God and man. He likened the Creator of men to a bricklayer who lays good each brick in the wall to support those above it. God created each of us pure and innocent and fine and holy. The bricks were all created perfect. But the bad ones are you and me. We may have become faulty.

Now if a bad stone is in the wall, the wall is made less strong by this bad stone. How can you want there to be bad stones in a wall? How can you refuse to help your fellow man? We should be good bricks in God's temple.

*I have a place to fill. How will it be filled? The preacher
came down from behind the pulpit and said: "All those
who really want to be a good stone in this wall of God,
stand up." The entire group stood up, sinners and all.*

*Everybody wanted to be a real man and woman
and fill their place well. The last song was sung, the
benediction pronounced by the regular preacher. The
people all went home really praying that they might be
a good stone in the wall.*

*Tuesday came. Farmers and farmers' wives worked
hard until ten o'clock in order that they might go to
church. When the people in the community had already
or were about to arrive, the service began in fine style—
good singing, good opening prayer offered by a sincere
man. The visiting preacher opened the large bible and
read slow and concise as usual.*

*The people heard of the calling of Abraham and the
promises made to his seed. How God called Abraham
and how Abraham had often chosen the poor pastures
in order that he might keep the soul purer—how Isaac
was saved because of Abraham's obedience to God. At
length he explained this well and in detail.*

*Then calling down he asked all that wanted to obey
the call of God to come and shake hands with himself,
the regular preacher, and each other before the altar.
Everybody came. Everybody wanted to be a real ser-
vant of God—wanted to do His will, wanted to know
and execute the will of God. The last song was sung.
The Benediction said, and the people all went out to
go home.*

*The night meeting was fine—the best of all. The
preacher spoke of the feast of Belshazzar. He described
at length and in vivid detail the drunkenness, debauch-
eries, the terrible hilarities of that lusty affair . . . I was*

left feeling, really feeling, that I neither would nor could be so foolish as Belshazzar—so foolish as to wallow in those depths of sinfulness before seeing the handwriting upon the way and realizing that I'd been "weighed in the balances and found wanting."

The preacher said, "All who really want to be weighed before God and found fit, stand." Everybody stood. I wanted to be weighed and found fit. The last song was sung. All went home. Belshazzar was to be pitied and hated. Most of all, his condition resulting from his situation was to be evaded.

The next day came. The sun shone very warm as I chopped grass—hateful, worthless, pestilential grass— away from the tender tobacco plants. The tobacco was set very late that year; the grass seemed to be determined to kill the tobacco plants. Poor, little, tender, pleasure-giving tobacco plants were about to be crushed out by the rapidly growing enemy of mankind: grass. When the hour of service came, I had, as the others, come.

The meeting began. The regular preacher told of the good response made by the people at all the former services. The saved and unsaved people responded alike. Are there no differences? The people of God are a peculiar people. The people of God are not as the people of the world.

Now there was a certain man present at all of these meetings who had come a long distance and who, until this last meeting, said very little. He was a most profound believer in spiritual things; he had no faith in any worldly interpretation put upon life by worldly people. At this last meeting, the songs were sung and this visiting preacher offered the prayer. The prayer asked God to send the Holy Spirit into his life. He asked that the Holy Ghost be felt by all people there before going from God's house. He asked that all people should be separate from and not contaminated with the world.

The man prayed long and loud. Many "Amens" were uttered that morning. I became less interested as the man continued his wordy prayer about Holy Ghost, Holy Spirit, worldliness, atonement, and Up Yonder. The prayer ended. The regular minister stood up on the platform and said that he felt sure the Holy Ghost would come. I saw people about me shedding tears. I saw old men tremble—others I saw asleep—I saw young girls look at each other. I felt miserable.

The sermon was very clear, I thought, and very impracticable,. The preacher told of how Peter raised the beggar to his feet. He then told how Peter walked upon the sea—he was held up by the Holy Ghost—he couldn't sink. The minute Peter thought of himself, he began to sink. Man must be in the Holy Ghost area or he is lost. He explained it all. I was in a maze. I couldn't see it all . . .

At the end of the service, the visiting Brother said a few words; I don't remember what the words were but this is what he had said when he stopped: "This old world is a miserable place. I long to be far from this worldliness. Let us not think of worldly things. Let us think of spiritual things. Let us live as Thou wouldst have us live, then sever us from this world of trouble and tribulations and strife and pain and sin, and let us be with the angels on those shining crystal shores of eternity where the thief neither breaks through nor steals," and so forth. He quit his prayer. I was glad. I felt miserable. I felt as though I didn't know what it was all about.

The regular preacher stood up and with tears in his eyes asked all those who knew they would go to that City *of God if they were to die today to stand up. I didn't know I would go there. I didn't know I would go elsewhere. I saw all the folks about me stand up. They rose slowly. I stood up too. I did stand up, proudly, because everybody else stood up. He then asked the people to sit down. I did with the rest.*

The meeting was a worry to me. I had wanted a revival. I had wanted to be a sound brick. I had wanted to be fit to be weighed by God's scales. I had desired all this, but now I had a part of the revival that I couldn't use. Either I was out of line, or else there is more than one plan. I enjoyed the preliminary meetings fine, but when this real revival, as they called it, came, I couldn't use it. It was neither what I wanted nor what I could enjoy when once I had gotten it. The real was unreal to me. The warming up period was real to me . . .

There's a bit more here at the end, but I won't go on. It's at least enough to indicate my feelings about revival meetings at the time.

☙ At this point, some of the younger children in the group lost interest and either fell asleep or started fussing. The whiners were removed and taken to another more engaging venue. ❧

JOHN:

I didn't get as caught up in those Revival meetings as you seem to have, Arthur. I didn't get much out of them except a sense of relaxation and perhaps a bit of entertainment. I liked to go because it was a break from work, and almost any excuse to get away from the work for a while was worth it.

BLANCHE:

Well, it bothered me right much. The preacher would call first, "All who are sure you are saved and your sins have been forgiven, come forward to the altar." If I went I felt like a hypocrite; if I stayed I thought everybody'd wonder what awful hidden sins I had that couldn't be forgiven. Then we were also asked to go stand with the one who'd helped us the most in our religion. Of course I had to go stand with our parents or they'd feel bad. They forced you to be a hypocrite.

LUTHER:

I think I always answered the call, in my younger years. As Blanche suggests, it was easier to go than it was to stay home. I don't remember feeling so pained about it though.

∾ *My folks, Methodists, attended church nearly every Sunday morning. Mom saw to it that Pop and we six children trooped in to fill the third pew from the front, 11 a.m. sharp.*

Our minister, unlike the Rapers' ministers, read the daily New York Times and tried to relate Christ's teachings to everyday life—a hard task in the days of the Great Depression and World War II. In Sunday School we discussed Christian ethics, often reconciling ourselves that all Christ's teachings could not possibly apply to the society in which we lived. Nonetheless teachings of the Golden Rule made its mark: we strived to treat others as we would want them to treat us.

I did then believe in Heaven, while not fully accepting the concept of Hell. Such beliefs began to wane when, further contemplating Heaven, I thought what a bore it would be to have no conflict, no strident disagreements, everyone pious.

And what would you do up there anyway? Play harps all the time—forever and ever and ever?

By sophomore year in college, with teachings in cultural anthropology and comparative religions, belief in Heaven and a personified male God disappeared altogether. Now, as I listened to the Raper siblings, I came to realize that the strict religious dictates of that family's childhood also waned, once they grew into adulthood—but the ethical teachings stayed. ∾

LUTHER:

Arthur, do you recall ever going over to the Negro church for some of their meetings—the Holy Roller sect, I mean?

ARTHUR:

No, Papa discouraged it. He said that religion is to be taken seriously and that most of the white people who went there didn't go for religious purposes—that was the Negro church near Jud Shutt's place.

People came by the hundreds from Lexington and all around. The Revival meetings there were something of a show, I was told, with a lot of white people going there to ogle at what they saw: the enthusiastic singing, chanting, and shouting. I do recall, almost with awe, those fast horses with their buggies and carriages, as they came by Uncle Henry Wilson's place and by the church. It was something of a show, for many of them ran their horses very fast, and some of them had very good outfits.

I remember especially nearly choking to death by the well at the Wilson place when a group of us boys stood there watching the Negroes go by, and someone (maybe me) called out, "Here comes another dark cloud" just as a Negro passed closer to us than we had expected. Here we were, face to face with a stranger, with this sort of careless talk in our mouths; and, as I say, I nearly choked to death—and maybe well enough that I did, for as you see, I still remember it.

LUTHER:
Well, I did go to their services once or twice with some of the other boys in the community. I confess it was quite an experience. They were right more demonstrative than we, jumping, chanting, wailing, rolling around. They'd have a regular dialogue with the preacher 'til they'd end up shouting back and forth things I couldn't rightly understand. I thought it wasn't fittin'—that they were plumb out of their heads—but I kind of envied them just the same. They were so fully involved, physically, emotionally, and everything else.

RALPH:
I attended one or two of the Holy Roller services also, Luther, and I've wondered some whether that kind of service, had we been brought up to it, would have sustained our interests in Revival meetings a good bit more. Of course we couldn't ever really participate in them. We were outsiders, and we weren't ever used to so much emotionalism. Mama and Papa didn't go for that kind of thing; it wasn't in their backgrounds. It's part, I guess, of the reason they never did argue, that I heard anyway, or carry on much about this, that, and the other thing. Never saw 'em hug each other and say sweet things to one another.

ARTHUR:

If I may, I will make some comments with reference to my estimate of Father's religion. He was the first person I knew of whom I respected who said he didn't believe in the Virgin Birth. He said that to me. I asked him about this, saying, "This business of a woman having a child all on her own is rather unusual isn't it? How did this happen?" I remember saying also, "It's interesting to me that rabbits lay eggs only at Easter and jolly fat men come down chimneys only at Christmas. This is sort of funny business, isn't it?" He just said, "Well, there is a lot of other funny business too," and he went ahead and told me some of it.

I know as he became older, John, he became less flexible—well, he had less energy—but when he was younger, I remember him talking to Sid Raper, a Methodist preacher, who was ranting on and on about the Modernists. Sid had everything figured out; now he was what I'd call a Fundamentalist.

They sat there at the dining room table one night until about eleven thirty, with Papa batting down most of Sid's arguments about any religion matters that were mystical and other-worldly. Papa thought religion was ethically oriented and that everybody could profit from it in their everyday living. His religion in practice, I think, wasn't too different from Grandfather Crouse's.

It was in those earlier years that Dad first explained to me about providence. The fact is, until then, I didn't even know there was anything like that. Thus it was: one frosty morning, just before daybreak, we were down in the Cool Spur woods on a rather steep slope loading some spokes on a two-horse wagon.

Dad thought we had better take half of them up and then come back for the others, for there was snow on the ground and it was pretty icy under the leaves. But it was already getting late—towards sundown—so we put all the spokes in the wagon. Then he took the reins and called to the horses to pull it out.

As the horse on the upper side felt the load, he gave a jerk and threw the other horse off balance. Soon the wagon was skidding down backwards through the loose, wet, icy leaves toward a ten-foot-deep ravine, dragging the horses with it. All of a sudden, the wagon slammed up against a dogwood tree on the very edge of the ravine.

Dad caught his breath, looked the situation over, and said, "Now, Arthur, that's providence." I said, "What's providence?" He said, "Why that dogwood tree there, being exactly where it was needed." I inquired whether it had been there all the time. He looked at it carefully, and then, with a glance toward me, said, "Oh, about thirty-five or forty years, I would guess."

JOHN:
If I might point it out here, there are other types of providences. I think that Howard can recall being with me when we had three horses tied up in a yellow jackets' nest once. That too was providence.

ARTHUR:
Go ahead: what happened?

HOWARD:
I hadn't thought of that in a long time.

JOHN:
Well, I forget the details, but somehow or other we got a wagon wheel in the wrong place with reference to a tree, and so the wagon and the lead horse couldn't go anywhere. Besides, there were two horses and another wagon behind it. Howard had gone out in the woods to cut a sapling to use for leverage and stepped into a yellow jackets' nest. We had to stand there in this whirling bunch of jackets and unhitch the horses and get them out. It was great fun; I remember it well.

LUTHER:
Oh ho, glad I never came upon a mess like that; a heap of bee stings would make me sick on my stomach.

CHAPTER 5

Leave Evil Companions

ARTHUR:

Overall, religion had its conflicting influences on each of us. Its effect upon the community was also contradictory. It united the people into two opposing groups: the Moravians and the Methodists, who competed with one another for parishioners.

The Moravians had their roots in a richer culture because of their ties to nearby Salem. They inherited a long-standing tradition of superior musical services and also were relatively innovative: they were the first to build Sunday School rooms, hold Bible Classes for the young, establish Ladies' Aid Societies, and install heating and lighting systems in the church.

The Methodists, more rural-minded, belatedly followed the Moravian lead in these matters and did so reluctantly, mainly for the purpose of attracting their share of the churchgoers. Methodists resented the ill-concealed feeling of superiority held by Moravians, and it was perhaps because of that resentment more than for any other factor that they grouped together in self-defense to develop greater solidarity.

During our childhood, the people in the community lined up on opposing sides largely according to their church affiliation. Yet work exchange between families within a neighborhood, and often of different religious persuasion, brought folks together, fostered interdependence, and, by and large, moderated religious differences.

HOWARD:

Yes, and our parents, Mother being Moravian and Father being Methodist, helped in trying to bridge that gap. They provided us with the inspiration that I think has paid off many times over and over.

LUTHER:

I go along with that. They tried to live by those mottos we were made to copy down and commit to memory in the high school over at Enterprise. I have them in an old note-book here somewhere. They are sayings our parents set great store by, especially Mama. She'd recite some of 'em to us every once in a while when it seemed appropriate.

Oh yes, here's the list. Let me just run through 'em; children now-a-days don't have to memorize such things:

Hearken to Good Advice.
Learn to Do Well.
Be Always Learning.
Do Wrong to None.
Beware of Evil.
Never Give Up.
Always Be Prompt.
Knowledge Is Power.
Wisdom Is Strength.
Idleness Leads to Vice.
Be Cheerful.
Do Your Best.
You Can if You Will.
Speak the Truth.
No Lie Thrives.
Dare to Do Right.
Never Be Late.
Obey Orders.
Strive to Please.
Time Is Money.
Trust Is Noble.
Learn to Wait.
Be Polite.
Never Be Idle.
Don't Be Proud.
Strive to Do Right.
Leave Evil Companions.
Obey the Conscience.

Now, I believe these sayings, not all, but some, maybe rubbed off on us. Anyway, these are the kinds of attitudes that reflect our parents' belief in moral and ethical matters. For the most part they lived by them and tried to teach us to do the same.

BLANCHE:
I remember that list well. I think Mamma used it on me more than on the rest of you put together!

∾ *Such aphorisms had not died out by the time I was born. To this day I remember, and sometimes repeat a motto or two my mom tried to live by—not as short and sweet as those listed by Luther, but meaningful nonetheless:*

> *If You Can't Think of Anything Nice To Say About Somebody, Don't Say Anything At All.*
>
> *Everybody's Different—You Have To Accept Them As They Are.*
>
> *If You Have Something To Do, Just Do It.*
>
> *When You're Done With It, Put It Away.*
>
> *Save Not Want Not.*
>
> *A Stitch In Time Saves Nine.* ∾

ARTHUR:
You remember that story our mother told about the missing hams? It says something about the ethics passed down to her.

Her father Harrison Crouse noticed his hams were being taken from the smokehouse faster than he was putting them in. He knew somebody was stealing them, but he didn't know who it was—until one night he saw a familiar wagon backed up to the smokehouse door.

He ambled down and said, "Well, neighbor, thee appear to need these more than do I; now let me help thee load." That took care of the stealing. In due time, that neighbor paid up the price of the meat and also made very sure that nobody else ever stole anything from Harrison Crouse again, for a man who would act that way—it's hard to tell just what he'd do if he got mad.

JOHN:

There's one time I got caught in the act I haven't forgotten: As a teenager, I went out seeking adventure with some other boys who had a car. We drove considerably out of the neighborhood to someone's patch of watermelons that was reputed to be exceptionally fine with succulent, just-ripe melons.

We stopped and stole a few, and just as we were driving off we saw the owner standing by the side of the road with a shotgun under his arm. The other boys ducked their heads, but I didn't have sense enough to. The farmer waited 'til we'd driven down the road some distance and then let loose with his gun; some pellets struck the back of the car, but we were far enough away by then for them not to penetrate. The next day, word was all over our neighborhood that some boys were seen stealing watermelons. The victim didn't know who they all were but one of them was one of Frank Raper' s boys.

They called me the "veteran" for some time thereafter.

ARTHUR:

I stole watermelons one night. Upon very insistent urging, I went with two other, much older boys who I'll not name. We were on our way home from choir practice at Enterprise church. They insisted we get one of Frank Raper's water-melons, that they were about ripe. I said, "Oh, no," but I was a little fellow in my early teens, and they were grown men, so I went along.

When we reached the patch they thumped around and found a watermelon, broke it open, and we ate it. Just then one of the men, who was a very heavy drinker, pulled a bot-tle from his pocket. He sat there a little while, and he went into a harangue about Frank Raper, what kind of a man he was, and the things he was doing. Naturally enough Frank Raper's standards and that man's standards didn't match at many a point.

So by the time that evening was over—and I got away soon as I could—I learned another lesson: I didn't want to be stealing watermelons, and, particularly, I didn't want to be stealing them with the kind of people who did steal watermelons.

꙰ *Now such shenanigans seemed not particularly shocking to me. My brothers and I all knew about the money dish up on the second cupboard shelf next to the peanut butter jar. It had nickels, dimes, and quarters for paying the milkman who delivered every other day. I had a sweet tooth never satisfied by the measly earnings I made from serving at the occasional dinner parties my mom hosted. The dish tempted.*

I once stole ten cents, peddled to Lapham's grocery store, one block down, two blocks over, and bought ten tootsie pops

of all different flavors—orange, cherry, lemon, lime, grape—
unwrapped the lime one, sniffed, and started sucking. As I
bicycled home, a strong sense of guilt ascended at the corner
of Couch and Broad Streets. I quickly unwrapped two
or three more just to taste, then threw all ten away in the
roadside gutter.

A later confession made Mom laugh. She dismissed my
sin by saying oldest brother Paul, at my age, had stolen a
whole dollar's worth of change, bought one hundred tootsie
rolls, treated all his friends and, of course, got caught from the
reports of other mothers. Our mom forgave us both.

Blanche's husband, Aubrey, who grew up near the Raper
homestead, breaks in to tell of far more shocking happen-
ings in Welcome at that time.

AUBREY:
I've been sittin' here listenin' to you folks for a right long spell,
and right much of what you been talkin' about is familiar to
me since I grew up with y'all close by; but I'll tell you folk
what's the truth: there were much worse things went on in
some parts of that community than stealin' watermelons.
Why, you folks sound like the worst that could 'a happened
was snitchin' peanuts and gettin' pelted in your back-sides
with shotgun fire. Hell, John, Arthur, don't y'all remember
those bully boys, the Bowles brothers?

ARTHUR:
Indeed I do, had a couple of near run-ins with them myself.
Once when I was about eight, I saw one of 'em pick up a
plank and stick it out crossways in front of a young boy

coming down a steep icy hillside on a sled at lightening speed. I helped the boy who was hurt—not badly to his good fortune—but I was too little to dare do more than glare at the much bigger Bowles boy.

Then another time when I was much older, about fifteen, I guess, I walked a girl home from a box supper at the schoolhouse. When we left the school, I saw a whole gang of boys, including the Bowles boys, who seemed suspiciously up to something.

At any rate, when I left the girl—her name was Lona—at her house I did not follow the road but rather cut off across a field and an hour later walked into our house some three miles away. I later learned that the boys, about a half dozen of them, stayed at a bend of the road below Lona's house until toward morning waiting to "rock me,"—yes, throw rocks at me—as I passed.

I expected some retaliation, but none came, nor did I see Lona home alone at night again.

AUBREY:
Hell, man, they did much worse than that and caught hell for it too—got fifteen years in the penitentiary with damn little time off for good behavior. For a fact, my mother was a witness who helped convict them and their father too.

ARTHUR:
Is that so. I didn't know that. Of course they lived over nearer to you. Well, tell us about it. What happened?

AUBREY:
I expect the crime happened after you'd gone away to college, Arthur.

As I recollect it, it started when the two Bowles boys and their father went to go hunting on the Cramer land; the Cramers were near neighbors of ours. Old man Cramer heard them, saw them with their guns and all. The Bowles were much taken up with their guns and their hunting, usually on somebody else's land. Cramer, who had little use for the Bowles anyway, ordered them off his land. There was a heap of argument and right much foul-mouthing with the upshot of it being that the Bowles left in a fair huff, with a real grudge on, you might say.

A little later on, they bullied Cramer's boy who was about thirteen or fourteen at the time, I'd guess. Cramer then, in retaliation, put out a "Peace Bond" on the Bowles boys.

What's a Peace Bond? someone asked. Aubrey explained: It's a court order demanding deposit of a sum of money as guarantee that the perpetrator will not threaten another person. A violation would result in giving up the bond money and could lead to arrest.

Well, the boys got so mad back at him they grabbed Cramer's boy one day on his way home from school, dragged him into the woods, held him down, and castrated him with a pocket knife. They only got but one testicle, but that was bad enough.

Of course the Bowles denied they'd done it, said they'd never been near the place where it happened. Even the father lied for them, said they'd been clear out of the neighborhood that day. Cramer took them all to court, and it was my mother's testimony that helped convict them . . . She'd seen the older Bowles boy, Harold, driving by our house that day soon after the incident took place. The two boys got fifteen years apiece and the father, ten.

LUTHER:
That's a right gory story, Aubrey. I'd heard something about it, second-, third-hand, so to speak, but I didn't have the details as intimately as you. The Cramer boy recovered, I believe, grew up to father a family.

AUBREY:
He did, as I recall.

Some of you Rapers must remember an even grimmer incident that took place a few years later on. Leastwise you ought to have heard tell about it from your daddy 'cause he did jury duty for this one. Of course Frank Raper was a man of few words, so he might not of spoken more'n a few words on it, but y'all must have heard snitches anyway.

It was a damn bloody murder; Jake Schwartz got it in the head, not with an axe but a mattock. Jake was another neighbor of ours, and I'll tell you what's the truth, I saw him dead soon after the murder. I saw him, 'cause I happened by the Schwartz's farm that afternoon and saw a heap of wagons parked outside, along the road, over in the barn, around the house and all. I thought they were havin' a picnic, so I crossed over into the yard thinking maybe I'd get invited in on it.

I peeked through a front window, and nearly keeled over at the sight I saw. There was old man Schwartz prostrate in a pool of blood, stretched out peculiar like, with a mattock in his head, right by the fireplace in the parlor there—blood ran all the way across the fireplace and along the wall.

They determined that his own son Joe had done it. It seems Joe wanted money to go to some special show that'd come to town. He didn't have any himself. He asked his daddy for it—he knew his daddy had $200 stashed away.

His daddy wouldn't give him any. I guess the boy needed only about two bits, or four, maybe; might have wanted to take a girl to the show, I don't know.

Well then, the story goes Joe took a near brand new shovel from the tool shed and went over to the neighbor's house to try and sell it and maybe get the money that way. The neighbor, Sid Moss, said he'd pay four dollars for it but didn't have the money right then. So Joe went back home—must have stopped by the shed—put back the shovel, picked up the mattock, then went after his daddy with it in the parlor there. He found the money. Whether he ever went to the show or not, I can't say. The fact is, they did catch up with him, sent him up to the state penitentiary for a thirty-year stretch, but he got out in ten.

℘ *I'd known Aubrey for over fifteen years and never heard him tell a story like this before. I suppose equal horrors occurred in my hometown, but if they did, our parents never told us about it. The only thing this brings to mind is the time when (going back to the dish on the second cupboard shelf) I stole four quarters to go to the carnival in town with the neighbors.*

I ran across the street to ask Mom if I could go and could she give me the money for it, but she wasn't there, and this was a rare opportunity—the carnival would pack up and leave early next morning. Well, big brother Paul caught me at it. It's the only time anyone laid a hand on me. He turned me over his knee and gave me the only spanking I ever experienced. I didn't get to the carnival; I put the quarters back.

As for death by violence, brother Luther told me he found blood on the front seat of our Franklin car one morning when he was a boy of eight. He asked Dad about it, and Dad said it came from an acquaintance, a merchant in town, who shot himself in the woods up the street when he learned he'd lost everything in the big stock market crash of 1929. Dad found him, tried to rescue him, but it was too late. ❧

ARTHUR:
These are things, Aubrey, we didn't know much about—very little in fact—but they did happen to take place along about the time we were growing up. And they were, unfortunately, a part of our community. As you say, I expect our father knew all about these events, but he more than likely didn't want to let on to us children about them.

How about some pleasanter thoughts. Ralph, can we depend on you to change the subject?

CHAPTER 6

Do Wrong to None

Ralph:

I remember the cool fresh water from the Cool Spur
    Spring
Down in the woods about a quarter of a mile away
And, on occasions
When we could not rely on the well for water
We went to the Spring
And got the most delectable water I have ever tasted
Dipping it right out of the Spring
In which you could invariably see a frog, tadpole,
    salamander, or something.

I remember the tree down in the draw by the barn
With a hole in one side about twenty feet up from the
    ground
Where we once found an old mother 'possum
And a litter of little ones.

I remember setting muskrat traps and rabbit gums in
*   late fall and early winter*
In and around the edges of the woods and thickets
Getting up before the break of day and making the
*   rounds*
Sometimes on horseback
But mostly on foot.

I remember the dining room and the seating
*   arrangement*
With Mother on the corner near the kitchen
And the youngest child next to her
The next youngest next, and so forth
Up that side and down the back
And Papa at the head of the table ready to pinch the
*   ones nearest him*
Anytime they started talking, when he thought they
*   should be listening.*

HOWARD:

This business of sitting at the end of the table: I was the fifth youngster, and when Cletus left, I was on that left hand side next to my Daddy on the end. Then, a little later, when John and Kenneth with Mother began to push up, they pushed me over to the big boys' side. Well, I was the closest one to Papa on the right side then, so I got a double dose of pinching.

LUTHER:

You know, it was interesting how he would pinch you—

he wouldn't say a word, not a word would he say—but he really kept order around that table by pinching the boy next to him.

JOHN:
Then there was his one word cure for hiccups. He'd look you dead in the eye with deadpan authority and quietly say: "Shutup." No matter how hard I tried to dredge up another hiccup, I never could. No one else since has had that kind of power over me.

KENNETH:
While we're talking about Father and the table, you may recall that he always ate the gizzard. Many, many years later, he said, "I really don't like the gizzard, but a chicken has only one."

LUTHER:
And Mother used to eat the backs, and always said she liked them best . . . she was doing it to give us the better pieces all the time, I guess.

KENNETH:
Well, our father, I'm sure, was eating this gizzard to sort of keep order around the place—because there was only one.

My dad really liked the gizzard. That's why he ate it. Mom preferred the heart. When I tried the heart and said I liked it, Mom denied herself and let me have it.

As for order around the dinner table, sometimes the boys would start teasing and pick on one another. When Mother told them to stop, and they didn't, she sometimes just lost it. She'd jump up from the table with tears in her eyes, saying, "I spent most the morning getting this meal, and if you boys can't behave I'm going to my room and staying there!" We then felt so bad we'd finish our meal in silence. These were likely the times when her hyperthyroid problem flared, and she really wanted to be alone. ∾

ARTHUR:

Luther, your interest in chickens goes back a bit, at least to Churchland High School. Remember, we lived in a three-story fat-pine dormitory operated by 'Uncle' Mock Koontz and his daughters. I recall that you, my brother, had a very good way of having something tasty to eat there along about midnight.

You and 'Uncle' Mock invited me out one night to feed the chickens. 'Uncle' Mock fed the chickens—and you caught one, sneaked it under your shirt. That night, on the third floor, we and some of the other boarding students got the old pot-bellied stove real hot, dressed the chicken, disposed of the refuse in the hot fire, and then stewed up that bird and ate it, with milk-gravy, as I remember. Well, the thing that still surprised me is that stolen chicken should have tasted so good.

LUTHER:

I never got but one chicken, and that was because two of the fellows tried and they failed. We kidded them so mercilessly that I was dared to go get the chicken myself. So I went and got the chicken, and we killed it up on the school ground.

The next morning, the Superintendent, Mr. Hasty, was

seen standing over this blood spot. When he dismissed chapel, if you remember, Arthur, he announced that he would like to see Luther Raper.

He called me into the office, and of course I was just as guilty as sin, and he said to me, "Luther, do you by chance know anything about the chicken that was killed last night?" I said, "Yes, I do." And he said, "Do you know who did it?" I said, "I did it." He said, "Yes, I knew you would be honest. "Well," I said, "Mr. Hasty, it wasn't so bad, for 'Uncle' Mock Koontz came up and helped us eat it. It was good chicken. He came up at 1:00 a.m., for he had smelled it. He came into the room saying: "I smell chicken cooking, and I like it too."

One more word, because I wasn't a thief. It was customary in this high school that the classes every year have a feast of some kind. This time I got sucked in on it. I was dared to go get the chicken, and it was easy for me to catch a chicken. I had caught them all my life.

RALPH:
Beginning at age two.

LUTHER:
Yes, beginning at age two, I'm afraid. We used to raise little chicks along with hens in coops made out of tobacco sticks; do you remember? And on top of the coops, to keep the chickens dry, were boards that Mr. Joe Woosley, the hired man, had split out of oak timber.

I must have been too little to know what I was doing, but Mother claims she caught me one day taking the boards off the top and, as the little chicks would jump up to come out, mowing their heads off with a tobacco stick. Momma accused me of killing six or eight of them as they came out before she caught me. I don't remember having done it, but I was guilty, I'm sure.

BLANCHE:
And Luther, don't forget the time you painted one green.

LUTHER:
I'd rather forget.

ᔥ *Luther's story reminds me of a time in my childhood when my brothers and I would go frog hunting down at our farm. With flashlights, clubs, and gunnysacks in hand, we stalked the cute little green hoppers at night when they were out looking for an evening meal. We stunned and sacked them for slaughter next day.*

That ritual took place on the roof of our chicken coop. As my brothers instructed, we'd hold each frog at the edge of the roof, slice off its torso, front legs attached, and watch it jump off the roof for chicken feed in the yard below. The chickens liked that.

Then Mom cooked the plump hind legs in nicely seasoned butter for our noontime meal. We liked that.

I have felt sorry about it ever since. ᔥ

ARTHUR:
Getting back to the stolen chicken—

LUTHER:
I'd rather not.

ARTHUR:
Nevertheless, this man Mr. Hasty whom you talked about putting you on the spot about the chicken, was he not one of the best friends you ever had?

LUTHER:
One of the best friends I ever had.

ARTHUR:
And most of the friendship matured after that.

LUTHER:
Yes, well, he used to say I was honest. But now y'all oughtn't challenge just me on this chicken business. I know for a fact you little boys played some tricks on 'em just to amuse yourselves.

KENNETH:
You mean like when John and I would tie a kernel of corn to a string, feed the chicken the corn, hold fast the string and, once she'd swallowed, lead her along?

JOHN:
I expect it was what Luther was talking about.

KENNETH:
I remember a little exchange between Mama and Ralph, and I'm wondering who, in this case, was responsible—maybe you, Luther, or some dogs, or just plain providence. I was in the kitchen one morning when Ralph came in and Momma asked, "Did you feed the chickens?" Ralph answered, "Yes, but it makes no difference; they're all dead."

LUTHER:

Now don't go accusing me of killing all the chickens; I think I'd learned my lesson well by the time that came to pass.

ARTHUR:

Well, if dogs did it they could have been ours. I think I have a little remembrance about dogs and chickens. Dad, when I first remember, did a lot of hunting—particularly at night, 'possums largely. I don't think we needed the food, particularly because I can't remember eating 'possum but one or two times, but it was a pastime, and he and other men would get together and go hunting—so there were some dogs around our place.

I must have been not more than four years old. This was the picture when we came home one Sunday afternoon from Grandfather Crouse's . . . whether we were in a buggy or carriage I don't remember.

It was about sundown when we drove in the yard and here were the chickens, practically all we had, piled up around the red maple tree just to the right of the short path between the back door steps and the well. There were feathers scattered around. Dad took a look at the situation, saw that his dogs had killed the chickens and made sport of piling them up close to the back door. Well that was the end of the dogs. There were, in fact, no other dogs at our house that I remember for the next couple of decades.

Now as I tell this, I sort of have a half feeling that this is a dream, but on the other hand, I think it is a fact.

LUTHER:

I vaguely recollect it. I'd count it for a fact.

JOHN:

Two decades may be about right. We had no dogs when I was little, but there was a succession of three later on when I was going to high school. None was for hunting; they were strays that wandered in on us. The first was a Highland Scotch Terrier, cute as a bug's ear, all white fluff and—

BLANCHE:

John, may I ask a question?

JOHN:

You already have.

BLANCHE:

And if I weren't such a nice sister, and if you weren't a favorite brother, I'd kick your shins for that. Some folks never grow up quite!

I'll ask my question anyway. What was that dog's name? Something beginning with B: "Bugger?... Boogey?" Something like that.

JOHN:

We called him "Booger." Ralph found him one day, sitting by a lonely road, way off in the wilderness near a beach he'd been to.

RALPH:

That's right; there wasn't a soul around and hadn't been for some miles. He looked so lost. I stopped the car, opened the door, the dog hopped right in just as if he'd been waiting for me. He was content to remain at our house thereafter.

JOHN:

The last dog we had was a mongrel. I loved him dearly, but I can't remember his name. I think I can't remember it on purpose, because of his terrible ending:

A certified mad dog had wandered down our road and bitten him. Rather than see him develop rabies, I took him out to the pasture. I told him to sit and wait; I backed off; he looked at me expectantly with pleading eyes, wagging tail, waiting for the usual word of release so he could come and be petted.

I shot him in the head instead. It was one of the most tearing things I ever had to do.

BLANCHE:

John, I know you did love that dog. This must have happened when I was away at college. No one ever told me you had to shoot him, I'm glad I wasn't home that day.

ॐ *John grew up to love having dogs. He preferred wire-haired fox terriers for their bounciness and the challenge of training them. Perhaps as the youngest and seemingly most disciplined of all the siblings, he sought some satisfaction in trying to control winsome, irrepressible pets. Hearing this story about having to shoot his own beloved pet puts a lump in my throat. I love him the more for suffering so and having such courage.* ॐ

ARTHUR

I've been thinking all evening while we've been talking here how much we've lost in Cletus's death. Why, he was the liveliest of the bunch at our last reunion; always had something of a whimsical nature to say, comment upon. He put a different twist on things somehow; looked at things just a bit differently from the rest of us, he being the oldest and all.

He's a grievous loss to us. Naturally enough, we can't speak for him, only about him. I've a word or two here written down about Cletus and the War. Let me start with that:

I remember, of course, when Cletus voluntarily went off to World War I, when Luther was later called up for the draft and was accepted, and when I, too, had been called up to report. All of this left Dad greatly saddened. He didn't believe we had any business fighting over there.

Word came back from Cletus in Europe now and again. Despite Dad's feeling—and the feelings of many another like him, I might add—we were all committed to seeing this thing through.

What relief there was when it was over! It happened just before I had to report to the Army. I was on my way to Winston-Salem with a load of hay and was going up the Sol Miller hill from South Fork creek some five or six miles from Winston-Salem just at daybreak, and the wind must have been from the north, for, of a sudden, I heard the bells and whistles at Winston-Salem break forth and continue for several minutes. I was by myself and thought surely this meant the War was over. It did.

After a time, Cletus came home. He had been gassed. The effects of that stayed with him over the years and doubtless didn't help him any when he later developed a heart condition.

Cletus and Billy.

He never wanted to talk about his experiences; and really, how does one talk about it? And how does a family adjust to one of its members having borne the peril of the conflict? And even beyond this, how does a family adjust to the fact that it was Cletus and Gertrude's only son Billy who was the only direct family casualty in World War II? In the face of facts like these, I can only stand deferentially, humble, silent.

 ℘ *I think of my mother's youngest brother Luther who also volunteered for the army in World War I. News of his death arrived just after Armistice Day. His father, like Frank, strongly opposed that war, having earlier practiced law midst a Midwest community of honest German immigrants who always paid their bills on time.*

Luther grew up motherless—his mother, my grandmother, died of tuberculosis when he was merely two. Grandfather favored Luther as his most promising child. He never got over his death, in what he thought was a tragic, thoughtless war.

Four of my five older brothers served in World War II. Unlike Billy, they all came home, scarred but safe. ℘

HOWARD:

Arthur, there is one thing you mentioned incorrectly about going to Winston-Salem with a load of hay on this particular day, the first Armistice Day, for I was with you on that load of hay—whether you remember that redheaded guy or not.

I remember when we got to Winston-Salem and reached the place where the load of hay, already having been sold, was to be delivered. The livery stable was closed, and the proprietor had gone off with the parade. So there we were in Winston-Salem with a load of hay—parading with the Cadillacs. After a time, we prevailed upon someone we knew down on North Cherry Street to take our hay off our hands, and then we were able to come home with the empty wagon.

ARTHUR:
Well, I do remember the parade, but, sorry Brother, not you.

While we are talking about Cletus, I would like, for the record, to say that he was a very keen political and social analyst. While that wasn't his profession—he actually was very successful professionally as financial manager for a big construction company—he knew a lot about politics, sociological phenomena, and baseball too, a sport Dad wouldn't allow him to play on Sundays when he wanted to.

RALPH:
Just to keep the record balanced, Cletus wasn't always serious, hard working. He was temporarily expelled from the college at Guilford in his second year for hitting the president with a snowball.

Then, after he got back from the War, he and another fellow worked for about two years on an invention: they invented a kind of balloon tire, but they were working in a shed rented from a big tire company, and the big company with their big lawyers got the patent. Some of us family members chipped in what we could to help with the lawsuit, but in the end, Cletus and his associate didn't make a dime—in fact they went into debt over it. He was so depressed about that it took him a long time to recover. About that time he met Gertrude and it was she, I believe, who helped him most, out of the doldrums.

CHAPTER 7

Be Polite

RALPH:
I remember the small dam that Luther, Arthur, and I built
Across the little stream down in the pasture
And that Cletus would rather read than join us.
One noon we saw him coming down
Reading while walking.
So we got on the bank across from his approach
Just beyond a fairly large hole we had dug in making the
  dam.
He came to the pond
Pulled up his overalls
Started to wade across
Stepped into the hole
And went completely under.

BLANCHE:

'Twas more a mudhole than a pond, but you boys could swim in it. I wasn't allowed to go and I wanted to right much—you just don't know how I craved swimming there—so much so that I secretly fixed myself up a bathing suit; I sewed it out of some old scraps of black cloth I found around the house.

And then I prevailed upon the littlest one, John, to take me over for a swim one fine hot summer's day, which he did obligingly. We no sooner got there when my homemade suit began to rip, first on the left side, then up the back; it began to disintegrate altogether—before I even got into the water. I had to sneak home in shame.

JOHN:

Providence, dear Sister!

BLANCHE:

More than likely. Anyway, black was an appropriate choice of color; I was in mourning.

∽ *Oh Blanche! I'm ever so glad I came a generation later. My childhood as the only girl with five older brothers took an opposite turn. Those boys had me doing everything they did: football, baseball, swimming, skiing, hiking, camping, fishing, boating. Our parents went along with that. I fondly remember my brothers' highest praise: "That's pretty good—for a girl."* ∽

JOHN:

Well I thought you ought to have gone swimming with the rest of us.

Young John in school.

Our father may have extolled education, but not in matters of sex. When I first felt stirrings for a pretty young thing, along about fifth grade, I was innocent enough to convey my yearnings to the object of them in writing. She turned my note over to her mother who turned it over to the teacher who turned it over to our father who turned me over a sawhorse and belted my bare backsides. That was the only sex education I got from either of my parents.

ARTHUR:
The only kissing I knew of that went on around our house was on the occasions when Mama would put Blanche to bed, when she was little, or wake her up in the morning. I'd wished I was a girl so's I could get some of it.

BLANCHE:
I must have been little, Arthur, for I don't remember that.

RALPH:
I guess we all got kissed when we were babies but not after we'd gotten old enough to remember it. I never saw Mama kiss Papa or vice versa, nor did I ever hear 'em saying mean things to one another, like most folks do on occasion. Mama was fair at sarcasm though; she had a wit, and she'd use it to express her dissatisfaction with the way the farm was run. She'd toss a sidewise swipe at Papa now and again, but that'd be about the size of it.

∾ *I'm beginning to see where John got his sense of humor. He adored his mother, and adopted her sardonic ways. As we'll see later, John's father Frank, while a man of few words, also favored irony in making a point. John had not, however, adsorbed his parents' reluctance to disagree noisily.* ∾

ARTHUR:
Yes, and there was the time when we quit the Methodist church altogether because the Minister refused to oust Lem Dunkel who, a married man, was living with Dad's sister, an unmarried woman. We went to considerable trouble to travel the greater distance to the Friedburg church and take our business elsewhere, so to speak. Later, I guess, there was some forgiving, or at least forgetting, because, as Ralph and John mentioned, we ended up going to those two churches and Enterprise as well.

KENNETH:

You know, I don't believe his knowledge about sex extended much beyond a practical one. He, along with the whole community, had us boys believing that Felix Dipple fathered eleven girls and no boys because of his missing right testicle. He'd lost it in a boyhood accident. That's one of those things that was common knowledge.

JOHN:

I told that story to the surgeon who did my vasectomy; and as he tied off the right side he said, "That takes care of the boy one." Then later, the left side: "That takes care of the girl one."

ARTHUR:

Well now, I'm glad to see one of us, anyway, is taking a conscientious attitude about the population problem. You have two fine young children, John, one from the right side and one from the left. That's anybody's share at this stage of world history, I judge. Although, if that had been the case sixty years ago, none of us from me through you would be here talking. But as long as I *am* here, I think I'll continue to talk for a while.

Here's another piece I'd jotted down earlier; appropriate, I think, to the subject at hand:

When I was young, about four I'd judge, I went to Uncle Dave's one night, and when I got back home next day, the first of the red-headed brothers was born. Every time I went anyplace, except Grandpa's, after that, I asked when I got back home if a new baby had arrived.

I asked Mama about babies one Saturday, while I watched her make the usual eight to ten pies that

Babies, and future scientists, John and Ken.

morning, and she said, "Pigs come out of knots on logs,
and babies are let down from Heaven by a rope."

Then I went to Uncle Dave's one other night some-
time later, and Blanche was born. "What?" I said, "A
girl? Now she can be the girl instead of me, but it'll be a
long time before she washes dishes." I was the third child
and was supposed to be the girl. I became Mama's boy.
I washed the dishes while the other boys played. They
called me "mama's boy."

Before the third redhead arrived I'd gotten some idea
of how babies really got born. I was at Frank Perryman's
birthday party and we heard his mother hollering up-
stairs. A little later, it was announced that Frank had a
new baby sister. Ah ha, I thought, babies come from a
mother's hollering.

When Kenneth was born, I knew he was coming.
Afterwards, it was my job to tend to him and help Mama.

So you see, it took a while for me to learn about babies. I had to put bits and pieces together here, there, and yonder, and still I didn't know all the details 'til I was grown.

LUTHER:
For a long while I thought Doctor Bob brought the babies. While I was walking in the woods one time with another boy—don't rightly remember who he was—he said, when we passed a hollow in a tree, "That's where Doctor Bob got you." Course I knew he was kidding at the time, but I did think the Doctor brought the babies from somewhere.

BLANCHE:
I guess it was possible not to know that babies were borne by mothers because the women wore such full skirts; furthermore, they stayed at home during the last few months before the baby was born. Those were very modest times. Mama and I, I remember, were too embarrassed to go even to the privy when there were men in the yard.

One thing I learned about much later on was that one woman in the community had ten children with no apparent fathers. I can remember the woman's name, but I won't say it here. The Moravian churches wouldn't tolerate such goings-on. She was expelled from Enterprise, but she continued to go to Mt. Olivet. The Methodists seemed to figure where there's life, there's hope, even for the most sinful among us.

Then there was the affair between Elsie Herkimer and Freddie Dunkel, Lem's son. Elsie was the organist at Mt. Olivet. Fred was married, had a family even. Elsie lived down next to him. They'd go out together and do whatever they did in those days.

HOWARD:
You know what they did in those days.

BLANCHE:
I suppose I do. Anyway, she got with child. This happened after I'd grown, when I was privileged to know about such things. The baby was born prematurely—never survived. There she was, at church the next Sunday playing the organ as if nothing had happened. By then the story was all over the place, and some folks refused to attend the service on account of it. Others didn't know whether to go to church or not. One said, "Well, it's my church, and if the Devil himself wanted to come to my church he wouldn't keep me away." The Methodists were split on this one, but in general the incident was tolerated.

AUBREY:
Now hold on here, Blanche, honey. The Moravians showed a speck of tolerance, too—they had to, with the likes of my grandaddy, Julius Beckel. Grandaddy drank too much, and his wife didn't approve. "Julius," she said, "if you don't stop drinkin' you're going straight to burnin' Hell." "I'm not going to any burnin' Hell, because there isn't any burnin' Hell," he replied.

She took him on over to the Minister at the Friedburg church the next Sunday and told the Minister her husband didn't even believe in burnin' Hell. The Minister just looked away; he didn't want to get involved. I'm not sure he believed in burnin' Hell himself.

Grandpa Beckel was incorrigible, you might say. Sometimes he'd start to mention sex, and his wife would say, "Grandpa, there are children around."

KENNETH:

Some of the children—and I wish I'd been among them—got sex educated unexpectedly in a Sunday School class at Friedburg one Sunday morning when the regular teacher was ill. The Minister's son took over and told the class all he knew about sex, which was considerable, because his papa was a liberal and believed that his own children, anyway, ought to understand such things.

This showed a speck of tolerance from Moravian quarters, Aubrey, but it really expressed a private view of the Minister himself and was unusual, I believe. When word leaked out about that particular Sunday School session, most mothers and fathers of those children were shocked, to say the least.

BLANCHE:

I wonder if our parents realized how much we learned from watching the animals.

JOHN:

Oh, they must have.

BLANCHE:

Well I learned a right proper amount about sex, just watching the bulls and the cows and the turkeys. The turkeys went through a regular ritual. The male would strut about the female, all the while showing his very fine feathers. This would go on for a half an hour or more before they'd get down to the business. I used to love to watch them.

I wonder also if our parents realized how much we got from the Bible. Since they wouldn't even talk about sex I used to seek out the juicy parts and such of the Old

Testament—about the Israeli Patriarch; I read *Paradise Lost* all the way through because of all the gory details.

HOWARD:
Why, Sister, you surprise me.

Well now, I suspect we could get stuck on discussin' sex all evening long, if we've a mind to. Just because our folks didn't talk about it then doesn't mean we've got to make up for it now. I agree with you about their laxity, if you want to call it that, in acquainting us with the fundamentals in that area, but they did a good job in most every other way.

❧ *You know, my parents didn't kiss in public either. Nor did I ever see them holding hands. I did burst in on them in their bedroom one night when frightened by a nightmare. I couldn't understand why they lay entwined on the floor between their twin beds making funny noises. They shooed me out. I got some inkling of what they were up to only later when Mom handed me a book about "birds and bees" and we timidly talked around the subject.*

As for Bible readings, my mom read to us little kids every night before bedtime. When she chose the Bible, I, like Blanche, always preferred the Old Testament because of its ghastly tales, somewhat reminiscent of the Brothers Grimm, which I preferred to Andersen's fairy tales. ❧

CHAPTER 8

Obey the Conscience

HOWARD:

I'd like to get on into some of our parents' attitudes about life in general.

I always thought of our father as rather strict, and so was our mother, as related to our conduct and our behavior, such as truthfulness and carrying out a job once it had been assigned.

There was a difference, in my impression, in the way Father approached an idea as compared with Mother, in that Father looked apparently over the hill instead of at the side of the hill. His life was spent, as I see it, improving the neighborhood, whether it was better roads, building the telephone line, donating land for the church or the school; he went to the point of dabbling in politics. He wasn't very successful; he got defeated by the Republicans. He never became County Commissioner, but he was always at Lexington, at the courthouse, on the first Monday of each month, hoping for something he could bring back to our community.

Also, my impression was that he felt he had not received all the education he could have accepted and would have liked to have had. He felt that more keenly because of the association he had with a first cousin lawyer, Emory Raper, who practiced at Lexington. He would have liked to have had the opportunity to do that type of work.

The fact that he settled down on the family farm after his father died gave him no such opportunity; but he was determined each of his children should have an education, and he sacrificed that we might go to school. Never once did he say, "You better not go; we don't have the money." He skimped what he could. He didn't say, "Go get you a job." He never once said, "Go get you a job, and then you can go to school." Now, in my way of thinking, his ideas were on beyond an immediate goal.

Mother, on the other hand, was a little more realistic in her raising, about thrift and maybe orderliness. She was very devoted and a good mother. She was, I think, a Christian mother if there ever was one. She was as keen or as bright as Father was; she was the champion speller, if you want to call it that, around the neighborhood.

BLANCHE:
She surely was. She went to spelling bees, and she won right more often than the other folks. She had that tum-ta-dum-tum way of spelling things, and she'd try to teach us how with one of her favorite spelling words, like *antidisestablish-mentarianism*, or another one was *incompatibility*—I won-der if that had anything to do with your growing up to get so interested in studying incompatibility in the fungi, John.

ABOVE: Middle-aged Frank.

ABOVR RIGHT: Young Frank Raper.

RIGHT: Widowed Julia on her birthday, 1939.

Anyway, her way of spelling went like this! She'd pronounce the word first, "incompatibility," then spell one syllable at a time and pronounce it thereafter: "i-n, in, c-o-m, incom, p-a-t, incompat, i, incompati, b-i-l, incompatibil, ity, incompatibility."

HOWARD:
You do it better than I ever could, Blanche, but Mamma did it faster and better than she was ever able to teach any of us to do, I think. She also taught Sunday School classes. "Miz Julie" was always present.

"Mister Frank" was known to be the leader of the community and was probably the best-read man in the whole Welcome-Enterprise section . . .

BLANCHE:
Your comment, Howard, about Mister Frank being the best-read man around says something about our community, for, as a child, I remember no books in the home except the Bible, Sunday School leaflets, *Bloom's Almanac*, and a simplified version of *Paradise Lost* with authentic Durer illustrations and obtained by way of the evangelist Sam Jones.

Now as the big boys returned from boarding school they brought books with them, and every afternoon, when I could get away from the work, I read them, but I don't think Papa ever did.

Incidentally, Cletus was the first to go away to boarding school, and when he came home and talked knowingly about a lot of people we'd never heard of before, that was the first time I ever remember somebody discussing somebody I'd never heard about.

Never to be forgotten was one afternoon when I read some selections from Plato's *Laws* and the *Apology*. From the *Laws*, I remember the statement, "Men do not sin willingly; they sin because they do not understand the truth." And, from the *Apology*, I observed that here was a man who made death seem as natural and right as living. That same afternoon I also read a short book on comparative religions. It brought to mind my talk with Papa earlier about things in our religion we couldn't understand.

I discovered in the reading of that book that many people besides Christians had ideas about the things Papa and I couldn't understand, and some of those ideas sounded reasonable and good.

HOWARD:
Maybe Papa didn't read many books, but he took a newspaper daily, and the minute it came he'd drop what he was doing and read every word of it. Nobody else got a glance at it before he finished.

GERTRUDE (CLETUS'S WIFE):
So that's where Cletus got it from: the newspaper could never come through our door and be in the house for more than one minute when he would grab it, and all else would stop until he read it through. That never changed. I remember Mother Raper saying, "You might as well let him sit right down and read the paper, because you'll never get a lick of work out of him until he gets through with it."

ARTHUR:
Little wonder that was so, Cletus took after Papa in a good many ways, I think.

I can understand how scientific brains make a contribution. It's recognizing, then stating the problem; thereon after, it doesn't matter who takes care of it as long as it's managed by some fellow who knows how to do it. It's the idea that counts.

I recollect our father's remark when driving our first Ford automobile where you always had to be changing the spark lever and the gas lever. He said, "What you need do is put these levers in one place and leave them there." Well, we said to ourselves, he just doesn't understand. If we did that we'd break our necks going down the first hill and never make it up the next.

But you know these modern machines are fixed that way right now. Why, a $5,000-$10,000 farm tractor has a governor on it, and you can set the gas feed, with automatic spark. The machine goes six to eight miles per hour, up hill or down.

It takes a special kind of scientific sense to say, "Do this; this is what has to be done." Well, Frank Raper may not have gotten the hang of driving the Model T Ford, but he had an idea about what ought to be done. Even though he wasn't a scientist he had vision, imagination . . . He recognized the need, and that had to precede the deed.

That's the kind of thinking we have to have first, to start us off towards Mars or some other far-out place. The engineer boys don't have that kind of sense; they just figure out *how* to do it.

LUTHER:
I knew Father as a somewhat jovial type person, and I also knew him, John, when he had lost his strength. He'd lost his hope; he wasn't well.

JOHN:
Well, I only knew him like that.

LUTHER:
That is the reason I say, but it was definitely different earlier. I remember when he used to play pranks on us, practical jokes, and so do the rest of you, at the tobacco barn. You remember we used to play checkers with him, and that's how we learned to play the game.

When we got older and got to where we could beat him, he'd gradually let his knees come apart, and the checkerboard would fall—just before we would finish him off. He would sheepishly say, "Excuse, please." That was a typical type of thing as I knew him then. That wasn't true in his latter years.

RALPH:
I have some more rememberings I'd like to read.

I remember bailing hay from a stack at the Baxley place
And, as we approached the ground,
Finding a den of weasels in the dunnage surrounding an
    old mill stone
That held the pole in the middle of the stack.

I remember the tree down behind the barn.
And how it bent way over and broke off near the stump
In the calm of a summer afternoon
Not more than two hours after
There had been a very violent wind
With lightning and rain.

I remember taking a long stroll one Sunday afternoon
With a brother or two, and Eli's boys
And while we were up the creek
We stopped and went swimming.
The next day I heard Papa telling Mother to watch out
*   for Eli's boys*
For they had the "itch."
I worried something awful
Not wondering if I would get it
But when.
I didn't get it.

LUTHER:

But some of us did have to scratch at times. After I left Churchland High for State College, Arthur moved over to Jamestown High School near Greensboro. I went to visit him. Well, beds were scarce there, and so, when I spent the night with Arthur and his roommate, Malcolm Shepard, I slept between them. We were all resstless, and we couldn't sleep very well. I got back to State, and two days later had a letter from Arthur saying, "I'm very sorry to tell you, but the doctor has just said Shepard and I both have the "seven-year itch."

You know the rest. I went to the infirmary and told them I'd been exposed; they covered me with sulfur; I went to my classes, class after class, and announced that I had been exposed to the seven-year itch. I was avoided.

JOHN:

Arthur seems to have done a bit of wandering about that time, for he came home and paid the honor of giving it to me.

HOWARD:
There was never enough water in our house for everyone to wash in a fresh tub. I bathed after John, and got the sulfur treatment too.

BLANCHE:
Yes, well maybe that was one consequence of you boys having to go away from home to get your high school education, since we had no high school in our community at the time . . .

I'd like to say something here about Momma's view compared to Papa's:
With all the work Momma and I did together, we had time for long talks. I think I knew her in a way that you boys did not know her. Let me read some more I have about that.

There was time for talking, and, most likely altogether unwittingly, Momma opened up her frustrations to an attentive daughter. Papa was not as good a farmer as her father had been nor as her brothers were. She had tried hard to tell Papa how to farm better, but he would not listen to her nor learn from her brothers.

Sometimes I agreed that Papa should listen to her advice. Then very quickly she reminded me that Papa was more handsome than any of his brothers, a better talker, and much more interesting to live with; but she still could not see why he could not be a better farmer.

And there were many other confidences: she confessed that she dreaded visiting her brothers and sisters because all of them had better homes, better furniture, and their children could have more expensive clothes. Once, she told me how much it had hurt her when Papa gave five dollars to Salem College when his own children needed sweaters.

When the older boys began going away to boarding school, she was bitter. Her people had never gone away to school, and they had done well. She felt the money spent on education would never be worth anything to her children.

In the meantime, she had to do without comparative comfort and be embarrassed by the kind of clothes her children wore. Once, however, after Christmas holidays, she observed that perhaps, after all, she should stop worrying. Her boys were happy and not ashamed of their shabby clothes—why should she be?

The long talks we had together also revealed other bitternesses: she felt that Papa put his idea of family values above the needs of her and their children. Over and over, she recounted mistakes and shortcomings of the Rapers. In my case, reproofs often took the slant that I was independent and tomboyish like the Rapers, and I should be ladylike and embroider and make pretty things like the nieces on her side of the family did.

When dating time came, I was a great disappointment to my mother. Dating more than one boy instead of settling down with one was being just like the Raper aunts who had failed to marry. Nevertheless, she considered me pretty, was proud of how I looked in clothes, and took great pride in making me clothes that elicited remarks of admiration from many people.

Through the years, people who knew my mother have unanimously referred to her as one of the sweetest women they ever knew. Perhaps she felt she could unburden herself to me and depend on me not to tell. I was always rather shut-mouthed.

HOWARD:
You've changed right much, would'nt ya say, Blanche?

BLANCHE:
I'll pay that remark the attention it deserves—none.

RALPH:
Let me get on with some more rememberings here.

I remember the orchard in back of the granary
With a split-rail fence on the two back sides
And the alternating rows of apple and peach trees.
Their fruits never seemed as large or as good
As fruits on the trees at Uncle Dave's,
Grandpa Crouse's, Uncle Will's,
Or a lot of other places.

I remember the small field up the hill from the lower
*   end of Cecil Branch meadow*
Where Papa planted his roastin' ear patch.
And try as hard as he could
He never could have corn to sell quite as soon as Julian
*   Zimmerman*
Or get quite as good a price for it as if he had had it a
*   few days earlier.*

HOWARD:
Well, maybe it's what Blanche said. Papa was concentrating more on bringing education into the community than getting the best price for his corn.

CHAPTER 9

Never Give Up

RALPH:

I remember walking each day to and from,
First a one-room
Then a two-room
And later a three-room school at Enterprise
During the four roughest winter months, rain or shine
Until we bought a car,
And I rode to school.

ARTHUR:

When I started school—oh, along about 1908—we had a one-teacher, four-month school through the seventh grade, though the teacher herself never went beyond that grade. By the time I'd finished, a second teacher was added and paid for by tuition from the families of each pupil, excusing the four poorest of the lot. Shortly after this, a second room was built by the people themselves and a few years later, a third, by dividing the first, then a fourth, the last being financed largely by means of chicken pie suppers and ice cream socials.

The added teachers, including one at the high school level, got paid partly by public funds and partly by tuition. By now we had a school district, designated as such by the State Legislature, and were empowered to vote a school tax to improve our educational system.

Luther:
Arthur, you talk like that much was accomplished right peacefully. Well, there weren't any shoot-outs as I recall—the controversy didn't reach to that extreme—but the whole idea of improving the school, not even to make mention of getting ourselves a high school, packed a heap of bitterness among folks. Why don't you explain that part of it?

ARTHUR:
I'm getting to that. If you'll just listen a moment, I will.

HOWARD:
Hold on. How 'bout giving Luther a chance here, Arthur? He's older than what you are. He ought to be remembering as much or more.

Arthur:
Good idea. Go ahead, Luther.

LUTHER:
Well, I don't know as I can recall it in as much accurate detail as you, Arthur, or as well, perhaps, as the younger

brothers can, for I don't believe either one of us was there when the most heated arguments over the school, the consolidated high school I mean, took place. We'd both since gone on through high school over at Churchland and into college by then.

But I believe the alignments had been made earlier, back with the road building or maybe even earlier in the promotion of Liberty Bond sales during the World War I. There was a lot of competition then to see which town or community or group of people could get the best record in bond sales to help with the war effort. It was an expression, I believe, of people looking outside themselves, beyond their own personal problems. Some could and some couldn't. Those who could were largely the same kind of folks.

But Papa always said, "There are more ways of killing a cat than choking him with hot butter." Then he'd try another way. It's funny, he'd use that expression a lot around the farm too. When he couldn't get something to working, he wouldn't give up; he'd keep trying. He'd go on ahead.

He had another saying: "Let's get our ducks in a row." And that signaled everyone to get ready to do whatever it was he saw needed doing.

Well, there were five or six other families, including Aubrey's folks, who went along in the forefront with Papa. Others followed, but over and against considerable opposition. In fact our community was split right down the middle in these matters for many years.

AUBREY:
I remember right much about those fights over the consolidated high school. There'd be more meetings than you could shake a cat at. They carried on about that school for

three years anyway. The first vote was declared illegal due to some technicality or other. And to tell you the truth, the second try didn't meet with any much more success.

The folks *for* would call a meeting, hoping to talk the folks *against* into being *for*, but they failed most every time—the opposition refused to attend. A lot of 'em wouldn't even come to church, so you couldn't reach 'em there either.

I heard tell about one meeting they tried to hold over at the schoolhouse. When folks went to go to it, they couldn't get in; the door was locked tighter 'n a tick with a belly full. They contacted the chairman of the school committee, and he, being a loyal member of the opposition, declined to hand over the key, so the proponents of the meeting went ahead and gained entrance through a window. They opened the door from the inside and proceeded with the meeting only to find all the opposing folks, as usual, stayed at home.

As things went along, neither side gained much.

ARTHUR:
Correct, and when the attending proponents voted for establishing the school at that meeting, the vote was declared by the courts as illegal.

AUBREY:
Then on the third time around, the proponents of the central school smartened up a bit: they got themselves some expert legal advice, so they'd know the rules and wouldn't get caught on that count, as did happen in the first two votes.

The good people on both sides held a heap of prayer meetings. There were prayers to the Almighty and admonitions from the preacher, the Moravian preacher. Now he was *for* the school. He said, "It's time we all get out of the 'piney-rooters' stage. As it comes to mind I guess there were more prayers from the *pros* than from the *cons*, 'cause not so many of the *cons* went to church at all.

But anyway, big Bertha Bachman, she sat plumb against it. Though she didn't pray in church she swore, "I'll swallow whatever they build over there!" She like to about could have, too; she was that much of an eater! Miz Bertha was quite a gal altogether—stubborn as hell. She shunned doctors all her life and lived to be seventy-six. She said she took an aspirin once and it made her sick on her stomach so she didn't put much stock in drugs thereon after.

Boy, I'm tellin' you what's the truth: she loved the flowers and the birds—planted at least an acre of sunflowers for birdfeed every year; got about fifty-eight bushel of seed out of that acre. And she loved horses, cows, even the fish. She'd talk to 'em, claimed they knew what she was saying. She'd plant herself there by the pond in her big baggy overalls, wide-brimmed hat and all, then throw some bread crumbs in and say, "Come boys, your mama's got bread." And they'd come, they really would, thousands of "sweet fellers" and "babies," she called them.

But she was dead set against the school. Guess she didn't particularly cotton to the kind of learning that went on in a schoolroom. Maybe she figured you could learn more from nature.

Well, anyway, to get back to the election—and you can see the kind of cussed stubbornness the proponents were up against—the folks on both sides worked like the dickens to get everyone who they thought agreed with them registered, and I mean every last one including the old, the sick, a feeble-minded woman even.

That woman was made to get registered by the opposition 'cause they thought she'd vote against. But come the day before election Aunt Battie Zimmerman, who was *for* of course, had the foresight to drive up the rough trail to the poor cabin of that woman and bring her home to help out in some work or other—that meant she had to stay overnight.

Early next morning, Aunt Battie escorted her to the polls. She voted *for* after all. At the final reckoning, the proponents of the school had won by only six votes, but the rules were followed—except possibly not in the case of the feeble-minded woman—and that decision held up.

Now, the business of getting that school built went fast once they settled on just where to put it. There was some argument as to that. But once your father donated the land over by Mt. Olivet Church there, the folks agreed to accept, providing the school was named for the township instead of the parish.

HOWARD:
Yeah, Papa gave up five acres of his best land for the school. Fact is, all the people for it gave as much as they could, 'cause the County and the State would match what the folks in the community could supply. I worked all that summer to build it, as did you, Aubrey, and Ralph too. John and Kenneth were too young and the others had left by then.

Ralph:
Our family contributed 200 man-days of labor and 75 pine trees for lumber. The work of a teenager was counted at $1.75 per day, a team of horses at $4.00 per day. Excepting the land, our donation came to about $500 cash value.

Other families did likewise; there were about 40-50 folks in all, who volunteered 10 hours a day for the months of August through October. The only hired workers were the masons and the plasterers. When finished by mid-November, we had ourselves a $25,000 high school, eight rooms including auditorium, all in veneer brick. It's still standing there, second oldest consolidated school in the State.

A renovated version of the consolidated Arcadia school the Rapers helped build.

HOWARD:
Then I thought it just about the prettiest looking building I'd ever seen. As I drive by now I see it's kind of ugly. Of course, some attachments have been added over the years since: four more rooms, a gymnasium, butcher shop, auto and tractor repair shop, even a canning and freezer-packaging kitchen, where the womenfolk could fix their fruits and vegetables for storage.

ARTHUR:

Yes, and while the first of those additions, before 1930, were made with tax support, community fundraising events were needed to make up the difference. By 1935, communities all over the State had built up comparable school facilities much the way we did. As a consequence, the legislature, at the urging of the voters who now had lots of vested interest, levied a statewide tax to support the system.

Still, facilities for Negroes remained separate and un-equal, and local contributions at the personal level became less important—for whites anyway. I regret to say this didn't apply to the Negro population. Standardized school service throughout the state had been reached through the wide-spread interest and contributions of the citizens themselves in many, many communities.

The school opened the way to many other things, electric-ity, for instance. State monies funded a line from Lexington to our school, and farmers could opt to hook into it by purchasing poles and wire in the necessary amount. By the late thirties, after all of us had left, the Federal Government stepped in with its Rural Electrification Program and en-couraged the organization of an electrical cooperative, which extended service to outlying areas.

This of course brought a heap of changes: from hand-pumped water outside the house to electrically pumped water in the house; from wood-burning stoves to electric stoves; from ice boxes to refrigerators; from flat irons heated on top of the range to irons heated electrically; from scrub boards to washing machines; and so on down the line, not to even mention a revolution in the tools of farming. Earlier we had only hand tools: axes, saws, hoes, mattocks, scythes, wheel barrows, carts, and horse-drawn ploughs, harrows, wagons, hay rakes, mowing machines.

There was one exception: a single wood-burning steam tractor that went the rounds of the neighborhood at threshing time. A mighty thing it was: heavy, cumbersome, with great back wheels, hauling the threshing machine behind. What excitement when it came to our place, huffing, puffing, blowing a whistle you could hear for a mile! The sounds alone were worth the labor we had to put in when it came— the flapping of the drive belt from tractor to thresher, the whirr the thresher made itself.

And then the sights: wheat bundles thrown from mow to thresher-man, twirled and tossed heads-first to mouth; yellow wheat spewed out into sacks; straw mounds building towards back of the barn; water wagon clattering to and from the creek; barrels emptied of water to the boiler; wood fire sparking close by the barn; everyone ready to put out a fire; everyone getting hungry and tired.

You can see the importance of such a machine to that time and place even though it came but once a year. We'd do a day's threshing in cooperation with at least one neighboring family; we'd pay for it by giving the thresher-man a percentage of the wheat.

Naturally enough, access to electric power changed the perspective. Hand tools were still in use, of course, but new things happened on individual farms. Here and there a feed- grinding mill, an incubator for hatching eggs, and a brooder to keep the little chicks warm came into operation. Heated and lighted laying rooms meant eggs all year round instead of just in spring and summer. Electric cream separators appeared, then milking machines, electrified fences, power saws, and so on. As each of the implements came into use by one family, it was picked up shortly by many another family until most members of the community had most of these things.

But I'm getting ahead of myself here. Truth is, the first consequence of electrification was electric lights to replace the old kerosene lanterns and lamps. This had an immediate impact upon activities, not only in the home, the barns, but in the whole community. In effect there got to be more nightlife.

A variety of events took place at the new school, which had installed lights earlier than the churches. It thus became a focal point for social gatherings of several kinds such as fundraising activities in great abundance.

Now there seemed more things to want that had to be bought. Then home demonstration club meetings for the women, concerts, speaking contests, and parent-teacher meetings all became regular events. For general amusement, a piano was installed, then a wind-up Victrola. Gradually people contributed books for a library open to everyone. Thus folks got together in a new network of common interests outside religion, politics, and farm work.

A fellow might think all these new goings-ons would cut into the old activities, but that isn't the way it worked out. Fact is, improvements happened all over the place. The churches, for instance, modernized by hooking into the electrical system and expanding buildings to include Sunday School rooms, kitchens with hot and cold running water, refrigerators, stoves, and by beautifying with stained-glass windows, carpeting, new pews, some brick veneer.

Health care improved with immunization programs against diphtheria, smallpox, and later, typhoid. There'd already been preventative efforts against hookworm. The infected were treated with thymol, and all were advised to wear shoes. These things were begun with the children in school.

∿ Arthur sums up a decade of progress during John's youth. John got to go to that consolidated school because of community activism led by his father, then matched in turn by the government. Technological improvements followed all during the nineteen twenties, along about the time I was born with all those advantages in my place of birth, Plattsburgh, New York. My mom pushed for community improvements—the library, better education, public parks—when she could take time away from homemaking duties. She taught me the importance of that.

By the time I married John and became mother of two small children, we had settled in Lexington, Massachusetts, which then had a school system in need of improvement. I and some like-minded friends formed a citizens' committee in hopes of persuading the townfolk to pay more taxes for better schools. We had done a survey and found that our teachers could hardly afford to live in Lexington, despite second jobs such as waitressing and gas pumping. We made our survey public through talks to many established groups: the Rotary Club, Kiwanis, League of Women Voters. Our plan worked.

After a few years, Lexington became one of the most desirable bedroom communities of the Boston area, attracting young professional couples who wanted the best for their children. But the best of intentions can come with unfortunate side effects: along with higher taxes came higher property values, once again making it hard for teachers to afford living where they worked. ∿

JOHN:

You know, Arthur, you mentioned those immunization programs. They worked insofar as the children cooperated. I did not, to my later regret. The night before my class was to be inoculated against diphtheria, I happened to overhear Papa remark to a friend (with whom he was reminiscing about boyhood days) that he'd play hooky from school sometimes to track rabbits and maybe get in a bit of 'possum hunting. I thought to myself, *Maybe tomorrow would be a good time for me to do a bit of hunting.* I didn't want to get stuck with a needle.

I escaped then, but boy did I catch it about ten years later—in college. I not only came down with diphtheria—the worse sore throat in the world—and got stuck with needles full of horse serum antitoxin, but I got an allergic reaction to the horse serum and broke out in one huge hive. The hives were so bad, I forgot the sore throat. It was weeks before they could certify three healthy throat cultures in a row and let me out of the infirmary.

I wish I hadn't gone hunting that day.

∾ *Lordy, what else don't I know about the love of my life? He could have died before I even knew he existed!* ∾

CHAPTER 10

Do Your Best

RALPH:

Thinking back to the earlier days, when we didn't have those mechanical improvements Arthur talks about:

> *I remember various horses we had on the farm*
> *But mostly Daisy and Maud*
> *Not because of any particular qualities they possessed*
> *Either good or bad*
> *But mostly, I guess, because they were there*
> *And because of the very untimely end to the former*
> *When she fell on a sharp snag up the hill from the old*
>   *sawmill*
> *And had to be shot to put her out of her misery.*

KENNETH:

I remember Maud because Father really loved that old mare. He talked to her a lot, or maybe the word is "commiserated" with her. She was old and complaining, and that's the way Papa seemed at times when he wasn't feeling very good. I think he identified with Maud.

RALPH:

> *I remember one hot summer day we had considerable*
> *hay down*
> *And expected some rain in the afternoon—*
> *At least Howard said so and he was our weather*
> *forecaster.*
> *It was decided that Kenneth should go down to the*
> *meadow and rake hay*
> *So we could start loading as soon as we got there.*
> *The wagon made ready, we followed.*
> *But on reaching the meadow*
> *No Kenneth, no hay rake.*
> *We started back*
> *And soon heard a noise up the old roadbed.*
> *There was Kenneth, white as a sheet*
> *Lying with one leg under the horse that was lying on its*
> *back*
> *At the bottom of a gully about ten feet deep.*
> *To get there quicker, he had taken a shortcut*
> *And tried to make the horse jump an old tree*
> *That had fallen from the gully across the old road*
> *But the horse shied away and fell into the gully.*

I wonder if that could have been Maud . . .

KENNETH:
I believe it was.

RALPH:

> *I remember us boys wanting to go 'possum hunting with
> Eli's boys*
> *Wanting to use Eli's old dog to locate, track, and tree the
> 'possums*
> *And Daddy and Eli laughing at us.*
> *Setting off across the orchard and into the woods*
> *Not more than a hundred yards back of the house*
> *The old dog started barking vociferously.*
> *Within ten minutes*
> *We had treed one up a small sourwood sapling.*
> *We had a 'possum in our sack.*
> *This is just what I expected*
> *But for years, couldn't figure out why we didn't catch a
> lot more*
> *Before we came home some three hours later.*

> *I remember the perfect elusiveness of little quail and
> peacocks.*
> *Once Howard and I were on a hill in Jud Shutt's
> pasture.*
> *We saw an old peahen and her chicks, perhaps eight or
> ten,*
> *Across the branch near an old stump.*
> *As we approached, the hen scampered away*
> *In an attempt to divert our attention from the chicks.*
> *The chicks streaked for the stump.*
> *We knew they were there.*
> *We saw them.*
> *And then they were gone.*

> *I remember Arthur having the mumps*

And feeling so good
Mother had trouble keeping him in bed.
As a matter of fact, she didn't.
He eluded her
Went out into the yard
And ran around the house a couple times
Before she could catch him and put him back to bed.
The next day, she had no trouble keeping him in bed.

I remember Blanche would have girlfriends over
To spend the night,
To this day, I have never figured out
Why they would go to bed and just lie there
Laughing and giggling
Into the wee hours of the morning.

BLANCHE:
You weren't meant to figure it out.

JOHN:
I'm remembering something you did, Ralph, I never figured out.

When I was a teenager, you would drive into Winston-Salem on some date or other. Howard would go along rather regularly to see Catherine, and Kenneth rode with them to see Mary Ollie once in a while. I'd sometimes ask if I could go along.

Well, on one particular occasion you all said I could go, but I was a little late in getting ready. Howard and Kenneth were waiting out in the car getting a bit irritated. They called in to me to hurry and I yelled back at them to hold their horsepower or something of the sort.

Dapper Ralph.

You were there, Ralph, standing by the car, all dressed up fit to kill, with white flannels, you know, going out on a date. You noticed Howard's and Kenneth's impatience and said, "If John bothers you, just go 'P-s-s-s-s-s' at him; he'll calm down." I called down to you from upstairs, "If you say 'P-s-s-s-s-s' to me once, I'm going to come down and drench you." You immediately went, "P-s-s-s-s-s."

So I went on downstairs, pumped a big pail of water. You stood by the car, I think wondering what I would do with it. I carried it over and dashed it on you: you just turned around, went upstairs, put on a whole new outfit, and have never said a word about it since.

Such forbearance, Sir Ralph, made a deep and lasting impression on me. Until then, I was accustomed to reprehension for such behavior, and I was prepared to accept it, but you left me utterly puzzled.

RALPH:
No comment.

JOHN:
You mean to leave me suspended indefinitely?

I suppose you took a lesson from our Grandfather's temperance when his neighbor stole meat from the smokehouse.

Now other people were more predictable, like the principal of our school, for instance. He caught me throwing spitballs one day and made me make a peck of 'em for punishment. I didn't have enough spit left to make another for a long time after that.

The same principal apprehended some of the schoolboys who were stealing peanuts from our father's peanut patch, right next to the schoolyard. He sentenced them to protective patrol duty around the boundaries of that patch for all school recesses until the peanuts were harvested.

And then I recall the several occasions when Kenneth would start something, like picking up and throwing a terrapin at me, and just as I retaliated—as in this case, threw the turtle back—Papa would see me out of the corner of his eye, and I'd get blamed and scolded. Kenneth always looked so innocent; he'd shrug his shoulders, blink his blue eyes, smile benignly, and say, "What did I do?" Of course Papa seldom believed he did anything bad at all.

KENNETH:

Now, John, you're being unreasonable. Father caught me plenty of times. You only remember the times he caught you.

JOHN:

Well, you always managed to look a hell of a lot more angelic than I ever could. I never seemed to be able to master that art.

BLANCHE:

You know, if you all don't mind, I think here is as good a place as any to mention some old letters I found in Momma's scrapbook. They are from some of you boys while you were away at college or in your first jobs, as was the case with Arthur and Luther. Most of them were written on the occasion of Mother's Day back in the '20s.

I have one here from Luther:

Dear Mother & Father,
Today is Mother's Day, and as I remember last year, I told Papa that hereafter I would consider it Father's Day also, so I gladly wore the red rose that a little girl came carrying and slipped in my pocket this morning, she, having heard me say that you were both living. I trust all we children are doing the best thing, and I hope you both will tell us if you have any preferences as to our steps.

It has been some rainy here today. It has cleared off now and will be cooler for a day or so, it appears.

I wonder if the tobacco plants are most ready to go in the ground. I am afraid it will be dry weather now for a while judging from the way it has been for the past several years, when it did as it has this time.

Mr. Meekins and Mr. Hyrum, my chicken partners, are picking strawberries now. They are expecting something like two hundred crates of thirty-two quarts each. I have engaged you a crate at the last of the season, so remember this. They are fine now.

Love to all, Luther

And I want to read a bit from one of Arthur's letters conjuring up a family dinner.

Dear Mother,

Well, it's Mother's Day again, and for me a rose, a big red rose. And the red in my rose stands for something, too.

I must have been a lot of trouble when I was a wiggling, cringing, fretful little fellow—but you just knew that I was worth some trouble. How did you do it? I wonder. There are eight of us, and everyone needed attention, and everyone got what was needed. And all eight of us are just as happy, just as happy as can be, 'cause we still got you. I'll bet you get lonesome for me and the others away from home at times.

Well, Mother, what can I say? Oh, here it is: I wish all eight of these red roses worn for you today, could be at home for dinner. Yes, you would need to get out the big pots and pans and the fire would need to be built a bit earlier. But that would be all right, for John could peel the potatoes, Ralph would be glad to carry in the wood and get the water, Howard would think it fun to hurdle across the barn lot after the fatted hen; Luther and Rachel know how to work together while dressing a chicken. Blanche just likes to make cakes. Gertrude would like to demonstrate her Yankee biscuits, while Cletus talks to father about the next presidential election.

Don't you see? Dinner is almost ready. Now, you taste the gravy, while I give Billy the drumstick, and before you know it, we will be trying to get the whole bunch to the big old dining table. It's funny that folks who are as hungry as we are take so much begging to get to the table. Yes, it's all ready and nobody ready to eat except John, and the reason he's there is because he's afraid he'll have to wait.

At last the crowd has gotten together . . . the wearers of the roses are too full of chicken and everything else to further restate their previous important position on some topic of the day. It's remarkable, Mother, how your dishes allay wordy battles at our table. Things which seem so important and demand so much explanation at the beginning of a meal become insignificant by the time the meal is finished. Perchance a fellow full of good chicken does not worry much about the importance of the bread-line in Chicago, or the real significance of the new Ford car. At your table we are pleasantly filled, and we are satisfied to take our ease.

Then with slow contented steps the Tribe of Raper makes its way to the rooms farthest from the kitchen, all except Kenneth—he's got to stay here and help me wash the dishes for you.

But, I can't be there, and many of the others will not be there, either. So I'll just stay here in Atlanta and send my very best wishes across the hills, hoping my wishes will find you well and happy.

I'm glad along with seven others for the big red roses we wear today. And Mother, we desire nothing more than to wear them for many many more years, 'cause we wouldn't know how to live without you.

Remember me to Father and know that as you share your love for me with seven more, I share mine for you with him, whom you chose to be my father.

Devotedly, your son, Arthur

Family discusses issues such as the bonus marchers in D.C. during the Great Depression.

HOWARD:

You know, I think we got more education around that dinner table than we ever did get in school, before going away to school anyway. There was considerable argument about one thing and another, more discussion, more theory expounded than you could get in a debating society for years.

I think the older ones, as they went to college, influenced the rest of us. They got it started, so to speak. Looking back at it, we had the benefit, if you can call it that, of as many as four of us in college for a period of three, four, and five years. For a continuous twelve-year period, at least three of us were in college, and four, part of that time.

ARTHUR:

Yes, and as burdensome as we must have seemed to our father at that time, not just financially but psychologically as well, he supported us, in fact encouraged us to go to college even though he'd never even gotten close to getting there himself. More than likely he felt overwhelmed at times.

He did worry about one thing in particular: I remember Dad saying he thought maybe he'd made a mistake in letting us all go to state schools. This was about the time of the Scopes Trial. He did not believe in the evolution that was being preached, and he sided with William Jennings Bryan.

JOHN:

This bears out the statement I made earlier about the Fundamentalist business. He was a tremendous admirer of Bryan. In fact, Kenneth Bryan Raper's middle name attests to it. Father's admiration for Bryan was heightened, if anything, by the role Bryan played in the Scopes Trial. His contempt for Darrow was not soft-pedaled in anyway whatsoever.

Arthur:

Yes, that's true, but at the same time he let his sons go to the State University rather than putting them over in the Christian college at Durham. It was a hard decision for him to let you, Kenneth, go to the State College at Chapel Hill, but he did; and he did, if I may say so, because I said to him, "That's the only sensible thing to do; it is in harmony with everything you have ever done."

This fear of evolution was, of course, something that went through all the churches at that particular time, and Dad was fearful along with the rest. The decision finally turned on a rather fine point: they then had the honor system at Chapel Hill, with pencils and apples and other items for sale out on little stands by the paths, and as you went by you put in your nickel and took your pencil or apple or whatever.

I said to our father, "These boys who are over at this Christian college you are talking about"—and I named them—"they came over to Chapel Hill last spring and made a game, saying, 'Look here, you can get apples and pencils over here for nothing; you don't have to pay for them.' They put the apples and pencils in their pockets, and they didn't pay their nickels. As far as I'm concerned, the thing that you stand for goes with the folks who pay for their apples and pay for their pencils. I don't care if they are at the State University or where they are."

Kenneth:

Before we leave this thing about the interest our parents had in education, and the help they gave us, mostly moral, but very, very important, I would like, as one of the younger boys, to tell some of these people here something: We have, over the years, operated very much as a family, even though we don't write, and even though it takes the family letter months and years to get around. When it came time for me to go to college, these older brothers over here helped me a great deal, as did my sister, also.

JOHN:
And, please permit me to say that it did not end with Kenneth.

HOWARD:
Talking about going off to college, after Luther, Arthur, and Ralph had gone, I went to get my underclothes, undershirts, and shirts—and I didn't have anything left. By George, they had taken off and cleaned out the whole shebang. The next fall, I got me a corner over there, and began a week or two ahead of time to put things aside; I did this in self-defense.

BLANCHE:
Now as I mentioned before, neither Momma nor Papa thought it was as important for me to go to college as it was for the boys to go. Those were the lean, hard years of the Great Depression, and Papa felt that I should stay out of school and teach—I believe they were both hoping that I would find a nice boy from our kind of folks, get married, and settle down to a life like theirs had been.

I did teach for one year at Churchland, at the end of which time, I wanted more than ever to go on to college and learn all I could. When Momma and Papa realized how much I wanted an education, they finally agreed to let me go on to the women's college of the State University at Greensboro.

You older brothers, more resourceful than I was, volunteered financial help, and Momma made me expertly tailored clothes. She had a new sewing machine from a mail order house; she could look at a picture anywhere and make something just like it.

But, to back up a bit, those years you older boys were in college were proud years. At State College, Luther played basketball, worked, and paid his way and had money extra when he graduated. Arthur, at the University of North Carolina, was making grades as good as the city boys and won the Julian S. Carr Fellowship. Ralph, who had grown robust and strong—for he was the sickly one when we were children—won honors at State. And Howard, as he had always been, was a favorite at Carolina and was making his own way selling pennants and felt pillows, especially at the football games. In other words, all of you before me did right well for yourselves, and this gave me the needed boost to accomplish the things I wanted to accomplish—despite the handicap of being a girl.

❧ *Oh, Blanche, do I know how that felt! I, as the youngest and only girl in a family full of boys, wanted to be a scientist starting in third grade—I just KNEW it. But in the earlier part of the twentieth century, girls weren't supposed to do that. I, like Blanche, did it anyway, albeit belatedly.* ❧

ARTHUR:
You know, Blanche, I have a couple of letters from you to me when you were over in the Women's College. They're

appropriate at this point, I believe, because they convey some of the feelings you had about college life and the cost of it.

Dear Brother,

One of the prettiest afternoons I have ever seen, one which enhances the beauty of what I think of always as a beautiful campus. I have been sitting here by my window enjoying the tapestry carpet of yellow green blending into one of darker shade. Over the carpet, tall, majestic trees look down upon a lot of wandering girls who somehow look a little out of harmony with the rest of the silent, immobile, grandeur of the scene. Yes, I love it, perhaps more than I would otherwise, because it reminds me of the scene I see when I sit at home on the porch at night and watch the shadows and moonlit spaces of our own bit of creation.

Many things can be gorgeous but what we find most beautiful is somehow almost invariably through the eyes of a past of loves, disappointments, heartaches, reveries, happy days, lonely days, friendships, dreams. In its entirety, beautiful things we don't know what to call—happy? sad? or what?—but only know its memory is sweetly beautiful.

So much for my raving. Now for something else. In the first place I failed to set down the dates of the last check you sent me, the $10 one, so please if you have the checkbook handy, let me know the date. I had it cashed on the way home from the P.O. and forgot to look to see what the date was. In the second place, I want about $15.00 more, whenever it is convenient to send it. You see, it's annual time and picture time just now. Sure, I am planning to send you one.

Hope you are getting along all right. Write when you can and don't forget me.

Love, Blanche

And then there's this other one in which you talk about your plans for after college.

Dear Brother,

Had I told you I had signed my contract for Salisbury? Paulette Hubbard is going to teach there too. She came home with me one time. Perhaps you remember her? I suppose we will room together and so the only part I dreaded about next year is settled.

Of course, not knowing what living expenses will be, I can't say how much money I shall be able to save— quite a little I hope. As soon as I find out what my room and board will be, I will make out a budget to live by next year, i.e., I will say:

? for room

? for board

? for clothes

? for incidentals

? for payments

Then I shall live by it, save by it, and, when I get each check, send you your allotted part. I will be so glad to be able to pay it back, and it is quite relieving to know I have once before set a standard for payment and met it. And you can depend on it: I will do as much as I say. I realize that to do it, I will have to go rather slow in some respects, but I willfully came back to school and I will take the consequences and be as considerate as possible of other folks who are concerned.

I have thought many times of something you said sometime during the holidays: "When a fellow works his way through school and succeeds, he gets himself in a hell of a fix"—a statement I thought pathetically true, not only in its original application but in a broader sense as well: What is life except a struggle to obtain what is unattainable? What is the ideal for which we work, and scheme, and long for, but a beautiful soap bubble, delicately tinted with rainbow hues, lovely in

Aubrey and Blanche newly married.

the diaphanous reflections, but, at the slightest touch of genuine reality, evaporating into nothingness, leaving only a mocking distasteful smell upon the hand of the fool who grasped it?

But why so pessimistic? Perhaps after all, it is worthwhile. Yet, it seems, the things we look forward to, always bring disappointment. But why my moralizing? Nothing, except in a month I graduate from college, with a good record, and a high recommendation for teaching next year. That's all.

Love, Blanche

BLANCHE:
Fair enough, Arthur. I fear my ups and downs have been exposed, but they were to continue for right many years. As long as we're into my saga, perhaps you'll tolerate just a bit more of my current recall of that time.

After college and two grueling years of teaching in Salisbury, I was home again. Teaching now came natually; I was active in church work, and Papa and Momma were openly proud of me. Momma said I could talk and do things, and Papa heard people say I was a good teacher. Furthermore, I had finally settled down to dating the one boy both parents had been openly encouraging me to marry. As Papa put it, "the Charlie Zimmermans are our kind of folks."

JOHN:
So you wound up fulfilling the role they had in mind for you all along.

BLANCHE:

Moving in that direction, but not all the way. I had something different and, I think, more than Momma ever had. I had developed a quest for learning and a yen to teach what I learned. I'd found a way to pursue both with some satisfaction. Momma, on the other hand, was far more limited in scope. Aside from all the homekeeping, she had very little. She was active in some church work, the Women's Missionary Society, the Women's Christian Temperance Union, and Sunday School teaching; she participated in spelling bees; but outside the home and church activities, that was about all.

CHAPTER 11

Harken to Good Advice

JOHN:

You know, after you all had left, I couldn't wait to get off the farm and get away to college. But once I got there I didn't know what to do. I just played around, discovering those vices our parents forbade: booze and partying—got caught one night a bit in the cups, playing my trumpet on the roof of our dorm. I almost flunked out that first year.

Then you, brother Kenneth, came to the rescue: you talked up a course in mycology taught by Professor John Couch. Couch had turned you on to the fungal world, and you thought that might work for me. You were right. I began to see purpose in college.

Then, about the same time, I auditioned for the University Symphony Orchestra and played under the direction of another inspiring mentor, Thor Johnson.

KENNETH:

Johnson later became conductor of the Cincinnati Symphony, didn't he?

∾ *So that's how John came to be a better trumpeter than I. Although, while in high school, I got to be first trumpeter in the Plattsburgh Symphony, our local conductor was not of Thor Johnson's caliber.*

A few years later, the fates brought John and me together at the University of Chicago: He was a newly appointed assistant professor, fresh from the Manhattan Project at Oak Ridge, Tennessee; he'd worked on the effects of radioactive fallout from the atomic bomb. I was his first-year graduate student, transferred from Syracuse University.

We took up playing trumpet duets together in his lab late at night—an early bonding experience—until the janitor complained. We then switched instruments to quieter recorders. ∾

JOHN:

Yes, and Thor Johnson got me so interested in music that if one Professor John Couch hadn't gotten me even more interested in botany, I would have chosen trumpeting for a career. Although I guess I realized at the time that it would be a lot tougher to end up a second rate trumpeter than a second rate scientist.

KENNETH:

Well, you needn't have worried much about the latter.

John Couch, now there's a man whose enthusiasm for

studying fungi was so infectious it was almost impossible not to catch it, if you had any bend towards science at all.

ARTHUR:

And that's exactly what did happen; first you succumbed, Kenneth, then John. I think I have a letter here from John—he's one who has escaped this exposure-by-letter business so far. This was written when he was finishing up with Professor Couch, a Masters thesis I believe, at Chapel Hill. He starts out with a bleak explanation about his dire financial straits:

Dear Arthur;
Things are going not so good with me, the weather add-ing its share of murky existence, et al. (He writes in some detail about his debts and asks would I consider signing for a loan to a poor struggling mycologist, etc. Then he goes on:)
The way things look now I'm going to have to stay in school until I get a chance at a really good job, else I'd play hang for getting them (meaning the debts) *all paid off in the two years they cover.*

Mother seemed to think it was terribly foolish to stay in school any longer when I owe as much as I do, and am able at the present to do nothing about it, save ask for extensions. She's right, I suppose. On the other hand I think it would be more foolish to get out and teach school for the $70 per month the teachers of North Carolina draw. Either way it is a mess—one that I'm not prepared to make any dogmatic statements whatever about.

Are you coming up home anytime this summer? If so, would such a visit of yours coincide with a possible visit of Kenneth's? I haven't heard from him for months on end—I have written him—and I don't know anything about his comings and goings, if any.

The thing I wanted to say though is this: I'm just the least bit tied down here trying to get a thesis, oral, and written exams off during the next month and a half, so as to get my degree in August; I have not much time to spend away from Chapel Hill. But when any of the far-flung members of the clan get around, I want to see 'em!

In the meantime, let's back to work, letting our colossal egos guide us by the misleading expectation that we will solve the sexual mystery of Achlya bisexualis, and establish another great biological fact, which will take its place along with those of Mendel, Darwin, et al. I'm thinking 'pooey,' so you may as well say it!

Your brother, John

KENNETH:

Well now John, your work on the sex life of that water mold, first with Couch and later at Harvard with "Cap" Weston, did go far enough to make the textbooks, so it has taken its place among the facts of Darwin et al.

JOHN:

As a mere bush in the forest—it's of major interest only to other *Achlyas*, I fear, and they've known all along how to do it. Anyhow, 'twas great fun.

Let's see, you must have been at Harvard at the time I wrote that letter, too busy studying with Cap yourself to bother to write to me—working on those wee-creepy-crawly things, the slime molds. They too made the textbooks.

You know, I had no prospect of a decent job by the time I finished at Chapel Hill, it being during the Depression, so I applied for graduate school and a teaching fellowship at Harvard. I asked three professors for recommendations, and one of them, Professor of Embryology, Henry van Peters Wilson (better known behind his back as "Froggy"), said, "Hmpf, don't know why you ask me; I can't think of a thing good to say about you."

Later on, when I heard I'd been accepted by Harvard, I went back to the professors and thanked each for troubling to write on my behalf. When I got to Froggy, he answered back, "You mean to say Harvard accepted *you*?! And awarded *you* a teaching fellowship? Well I'll be goddamned!" Whereupon he turned around and walked out—never said another word.

Years later, just recently in fact, while chairman of the Graduate Committee of the Department of Biology at Harvard, I mentioned this to the Graduate Student Secretary. She was curious enough about what Froggy Wilson said about me that she looked it up in the files: she reported that his was the best recommendation of the lot!

KENNETH:
Well I'll be darned. I remember Froggy Wilson all right—cantankerous old soul; you had to practically tiptoe around his laboratory—but I hadn't heard that story before.

Let's get back to Cap Weston for a moment; now there was an act who could follow John Couch as few men could. Cap was a different sort from Couch—pretty much left a fellow on his own instead of breathing down his neck, but a very great teacher nonetheless.

JOHN:

Yeah, he could be cool. He surprised the hell out of me the first time I burst in on him, all enthusiastic about something I'd seen through my microscope, expecting him to beat me back to it as Couch always did. Instead he said, "Well, son, that's nice. You just go back and work some more on it, then tell me all about it later."

Then I'll never forget the day I came at him sputtering about something—I forget just what—and he said, "Son, must you be so damn red-headed?" Being a redhead himself, I suppose he understood the syndrome.

There are lots of Cap stories, but let me tell just one. It illustrates, I think, the fabulous combination he was, and still is, at the age of seventy-five, of venerability and downright earthiness—always in either capacity combined with exuberance. He would throw parties at his house, I mean bashes, and invite all the graduate students. The beer would flow, and nobody, not even the heartiest among us, could outdrink ol' Cappy.

On one such occasion, a fellow grad student who was in his cups, you know, raised his glass and proclaimed loudly, "Cap Weston, to everybody else you may be a full professor at Harvard, but to me you're just a goddamned tank!" Well, the next day, after the guy—his name was Davey—had sobered up and come to his senses, we asked him if he remembered at all what he'd said the night before. Of course he couldn't, and when told and reminded that he was up for his qualifying exam the next week—with Cap on the committee—he was visibly shaken.

He went trembling to Cap's office to apologize, and ol' Cap just sat there with a big smile on his face and said, "Why, son, that's the nicest compliment's been paid to me in a long time. I'm glad to know you think I'm good for something!"

KENNETH:

The Cap story I like best is about his service to a fruit packing outfit that hired him as consultant to figure out why the oranges they were packing had such a high incidence of rotting due to fungal contaminants. He examined their sorting and packing procedures and discovered that the source of trouble was the sharp end of a nail sticking up and puncturing each orange as it tumbled down the sorting trough. This of course supplied each fruit with a portal of entry to all sorts of bacteria and fungi that can make a living off good ripe oranges.

Cap got a hammer and pounded out the nail. He charged the company a fee of $25.50. When asked to explain the odd figure he replied, "Fifty cents for hammering and $25 for knowing just where to do it."

∾ John is the only professor I've encountered who had that kind of waggish sense of humor. Now I see where he got it: Cap reinforced a sense of whimsy that Frank Raper expressed before he became so ill just before Red's birth. ∾

ARTHUR:

We've been having some letters back and forth from college and all here. I have a couple from our parents around

Julia profiled with her six Moravian sisters.

that time. They never had a chance to get to college, or high school, for that matter. In fact the only formal education they did get didn't seem to teach them as much about how to write sentences as our schools taught us in our early grades.

Here is a letter to me from Mother. As you know, she wrote with an even hand and with few errors in spelling, but she never did learn to punctuate the way you're supposed to—this letter is typical, I believe:

❧ *Julia, the youngest of seven sisters, had formal schooling only through the fourth grade level.* ❧

Welcome N. C.
Nov 22-1927

Dear Arthur,

I'll, try and take time to write once again it seems like there is something doing most of the time. The Olivet Auxiliary entertained the Friedberg and Enterprise Ladies Aid Society Sat. afternoon we had a real good time everybody seemed to enjoy it nobody was in a hurry to go home.

Last night we pounded Mr. Goforth (Pounding here means welcoming a new minister with a pound each of cooking essentials such as butter, flour, sugar, and so forth) *and tomorrow I must fix for the Thanksgiving sale we will have at the school house. I'm to bake chicken pies and make some coleslaw They are going to serve barbecue too. Yes, I promised to make some pumpkin pies to send to the county home Miss Margaret Perryman takes dinner down there each year under the auspices of the Epworth L. I thought about sending you a box but I did not know where you might be at this time.*

Mr. Bivens carried a crowd of boys, John included, to Durham last Saturday to see Duke vs. Carolina game John spent the night and Sunday at the Hill I think he enjoyed it fine

Blanche will come home tomorrow and stay until Sunday. Ralph Howard and Kenneth will come Thursday night

There have been quite a few deaths around but none right in our neighborhood Mr. Charlie Snyder, Mr Cisero Doty and Mr. Sam Snyder were all buried

*week before last. Cousin Low Watkins is dead and will
be buried tomorrow . . .*

*Had a right nice crop of sweet potatoes got Mr.
Roger Berrier to make bins and finish up the basement. Shredded the corn 2 weeks ago, did not have
quite a hundred bu. in all. Have not dug the harvest
potatoes yet.*

*Have not heard from W. C. (Cletus) since you were
home last summer. Papa is not very well has a bad
cough and is short of breath.*

> *With love*
> *Mother J.C.R.*

Before getting on some more, let me read by way of
contrast a letter I have here from our father. As you'll see,
even though he'd gone through seventh grade—three more
years than our mother—he had even less understanding of
grammar and lacked her mastery of spelling. This letter was
written to me some two years after the one from Mother.
Martha and I had just gotten married and were honey-
mooning in a tent, a cloth house, as Father puts it, in the
mountains.

> *Welcome N. C.*
> *July 24, 1929*

Dear Son,
*We received your letter last week was glad to here frome
you for we were gitting uneasy about you and Martha
I hope you are Still injoying your cloth house I guess
you remember what you said about the cloth house at*

Arcadia You said it would Fall down Will your house fall down

John went with the Enterprise Band to Raleigh Tuesday and came back last night Stayed with Luther Tuesday night Grady Zimmerman had his trile yesterday he gat 5 yer in the State Prisen.

(I remember Grady as a big bully when we were kids. Dad's referring here to his conviction for embezzlement from a small bank where he worked after he was grown. Then he goes on about the boy he had as a hired hand at that time.)

About the boy $25 per month would be in line . . . if he is all right the first part if he will stay until John comes back which will be about 1 month . . . When you go to school and you must be on time and go regular or fail, that is the way it apear to me.

The Tobac is looking fairly well but cannot tell yet we will begin priming next week Eli and Fred Tesh has primed last week The cantalopes will be ripe in about 10 *days they are looking fairly well my watermelon vines is looking good*

R. H (Ralph), *has not got a school yet.*

The timber acrose the branch sawed out 43,000 (board feet) *and the pines at the School house sawed out about the same, We are trying to make hay and it rained first after Dinner, Son see it in bad luck, We are looking for you and Martha to be by in a few weeks and stay some time for we know when you git back to*

Atlanta you will stay for a long time. We are all well as common. Hope you are both well

Your Father

BLANCHE:
When Papa said he was "well as common" that was not very well. Momma, in the earlier letter you read, expressed the state of his health more accurately I think.

CHAPTER 12

Strive to Do Right

BLANCHE:

I want to take us back now to Welcome, if you all don't mind or even if you do mind. I have here the rest of what I've written and I aim to finish reading it:

> *Then came the days when more and more often Papa had the painful heart attacks and got "spells of blues" when he talked hardly at all. True to her nature, Momma panicked and lay awake at night listening to his pounding heart, afraid to go to sleep for fear he would need her. At last the time came when Papa's heart could take no more. With amazing calmness in the final hours, he talked to all of us and said among other things, "I've made a lot of mistakes, but I have always been true to my convictions."*
>
> *His passing was strangely reassuring and took away whatever fear or dread of death I had.*

LUTHER:

In Papa's last week of life, he named his pallbearers and had us write them down. As his attacks got more severe, he said to us, "I put Sol Hiller as a pallbearer. Sol's got the same trouble I've got; he can't help carry me." Then he substituted a man for Sol Hiller.

Immediately after that he said, "One more request." He indicated the spot in the cemetery where he wanted to be buried because of the land and the type of soil. And then he did something that supported a whole life of sacrifice for a family of children:

The Methodist church had a minister who preached at the youth, ran them down, and made a lot of statements a minister shouldn't be making and wouldn't be making if he felt sympathetic toward youth and youths' problems. That minister lived on the land Papa had given the church for building a parsonage. It had been some of our best crop acreage.

Papa said, "Brother (so and so) is alright, but I don't want him to have anything to do with my funeral. I've spent a life raising you children, and I don't think you are bad, but he talks against youth all the time. I don't want him to have anything to do with my funeral."

He told us he did want a former pastor, Mr. Goforth, to preside. He said, "Call Reverend Goforth and ask him to do it." Well, he meant every word he said, and we faced a kind of dilemma carrying out his wishes, but we tried, because he had confidence that we would.

Excuse the emotion, but it has always affected me that way.

෴ *Luther, choked up, has tears in his eyes.* ෴

ARTHUR:

We couldn't get Reverend Goforth—I don't recall why—but Reverend Sam Tesh was available, and we figured he'd do as well. I've brought a lot of papers with me, as is apparent by now, and amongst all is a copy of the Memoir Reverend Tesh prepared and read at our Father's funeral. Shall we take time to read it? It's a summary of some of the things we've been mentioning about Papa and is a good example of a statement in memoriam of a man well-known to the minister who made it.

MEMOIR OF WILLIAM FRANKLIN RAPER

William Franklin Raper, son of the late William and Mary Motsinger Raper, was born in Davidson County, N.C., December 13, 1863. When about eighteen years of age he accepted the Lord Jesus as his Savior and united with the Mt. Olivet M.E. Church. On December 12, 1888, he was united in marriage with Miss Lillian Evans. This union was of short duration when the hand of death removed the wife and mother and their first born daughter October 22, 1889.

April 18, 1894 Brother Raper was united in marriage with Miss Julia Selina Crouse and to this union were born eight children, all of whom survive the home-going of the father.

Brother Raper gave his attention to the work of the farm as the major activity of his life, but he was by no means limited to this field of endeavor. His sympathies and interests were too broad to be confined to one tract of acreage because the horizons of his life had been expanded. He was as a man looking and living in the next generation. In very truth he was a community builder both in material and spiritual affairs.

In his religious life Brother Raper was not the kind who would have sounded a trumpet when he performed a deed of service or gave an alms. He avoided publicity in spiritual things and while he liked to be inconspicuous, yet he was always ready and anxious to let the world know just where he stood on every question of civic rights or moral virtues. In the Church his steadfast loyalty and capacity of leadership were early recognized when he was designated to lead the Mt. Olivet Sunday School as its Superintendent. Other offices of responsibility and trust were tendered him as experience ripened. For a considerable period he was connected with Friedberg Congregation and was honored with membership on the official board.

He was a leader, a philosopher, a statesman, and a prophet, but not without honor among his own brethren. He was esteemed by many who valued his foresight and wisdom, and few men have contributed so largely to the all-round development of this community. He had the privilege of hearing many words of eulogy for his service to us and ours, but I can see him as he listens and then, in embarrassed silence, he would drop his gaze to the ground, as if in a prayer. In the succeeding years his worth as a neighbor and community asset will be enhanced.

Though in declining health for more than twenty-five years, his activity bore little evidence of this condition. For the past seven years his affliction had

Frank Raper's burial place.

been more in evidence, forcing him into complete
confinement at times. For the past several weeks his
condition had been critical, and in the evening hours
of Friday, June 17th he called his wife and children
about him and bade them an adieu, and quietly
entered into his rest in the early morning, 9:10 AM of
Saturday, June 18, 1932, aged 68 years, 6 months, and 5
days . . .

KENNETH:
It was a moving service; as Blanche says, the whole thing
was somehow comforting. There was the feeling that our
father lived a lot longer than anyone had any right to expect
him to. The doctor had told him he hadn't more than six
months to live at the age of about forty-five, the time of his
first attack, and he accomplished a great deal after that in
spite of his illness.

Then the thing about his funeral that has stayed with me most throughout the years was the playing of the second movement of Dvorak's "New World Symphony," you know, "Going home, going home, I am going home." It was played with exquisite beauty, on the viola, by John's musical mentor, Thor Johnson.

BLANCHE:

A few months after Papa died, Aubrey and I were married, and we lived on the farm with Momma. Then three years later, the three of us moved to Winston-Salem where Aubrey worked with the Duke Power Company. For the first time I began to question the rightness of some of my earlier relations with Momma. She was hurt and felt I had judged her a failure as a mother. As always she remained witty and congenial and made friends easily in her new surroundings. And as always she seemed to know just what to do to be most helpful to a young wife and mother. She and Aubrey seemed to understand one another. Both were practical and a little bewildered by their dreamy wife and daughter who had a compulsion for writing "poetry."

Momma and I developed a real comradeship during the final years of her life. Little by little, I took over the reins of the household and resolved that I would give her the best I had and demand respect from those around her.

Once again it was easy for us to talk together. Sometimes she talked of former times and former frustrations: "I'll be honest, when your father was spending all that money for schooling, I thought it was wrong. I saw, though, everybody wanted to go to college and I did what I could to help. Papa never doubted it was right to help educate a child," she said. "He had hoped one of the boys would stay on the farm with him but felt he had no right to ask one to stay. As the boys finished school, he was concerned because all of them were working for someone else instead of owning their own businesses."

Then she went on, "One thing hurts me: he isn't here for me to tell him how I feel. I was right about the education costing money, but what you children have is more important than just making money. You can go anywhere among any kind of people and you can do things and you don't have to feel ashamed. I wish he was here. I wish he was here, I want to tell him that I see now what he saw all the time."

When Momma learned about Kenneth's penicillin discovery—it was in all the papers—she was happy and more convinced than ever that she had been a good soldier in supporting Papa and her children in their desires for education. She had been wiser than she knew. She was proud of all her children and felt that each of them was making a contribution somewhere that could not be measured by the money he was being paid.

With pride characteristic of her family and its emphasis on industry and thrift she once remarked, "'There's one thing I can say; I never raised a lazy child!'"

ARTHUR:
And now I have here the memoir delivered by Reverend Needham at Mother's funeral. There's a deal more emphasis on religious doctrine in this service as compared to that given for our father some twelve years earlier. I'll read just a small part of it to give a flavor.

Memoir Julia Selina Crouse Raper
1869-1944

"The Lord shall preserve my going out and my coming in from this time forth, and even for evermore." Thus speaks the Word of our Father God to all who mourn the passing of this loved comrade of the Christian way. And this was the confident hope of our departed Sister Julia Crouse Raper, daughter of the late Harrison Crouse and Caroline Faw, born on Forsyth County, N. C., October 25, 1869 . . .

On April 18, 1894 she was united in marriage with William Franklin Raper and became identified with the life of this Congregation and community. For 38 years they walked in happy comradeship; toiling for, instructing and rejoicing over the eight children born to their union. Then on June 18, 1932, the earthly tabernacle in which Brother Raper dwelt was dissolved and his mortal remains were laid to rest in yonder God's Acre . . .

Surely it can be said of our departed Sister that "she looked well to the ways of her household," In this day when we are thinking in terms of crowning the "queen of the riveters" (for you younger folks, that's a reference to the women exemplified by "Rosie the Riveter" who, in the absence of enough men on the home front, worked on airplane assembly lines during World War II) *we cannot afford to forget that this dear one was the type of wife and mother that has made this community home-loving and God-fearing.*

ARTHUR:

Father's gone, Mother's gone, the farm lay vacant . . . not a son remained to tend it.

ARTHUR CONTINUES:

When our father got that T Model Ford automobile, in 1918, he drove it some. I remember he went down to Lexington, and when he got home to the barnyard, the Ford didn't stop when he said "Whoa"—whereupon it ran into a white oak tree. He got out, walked off, and said, "Now you boys run it!" He never got back behind the wheel after that.

He ran the farm, I suppose, not much better than he ran that Ford, but he didn't turn it over to us children when he'd finished, not really. He raised us to run things all right, but it wasn't the farm we ended up running, and that was

Eight grown-up professionals.

doubtless because he never liked working the farm himself, and didn't expect us to either. He helped us seek elsewhere for broader, and what he thought might be better, opportunities.

Mother was out in the front yard one day when a passing motorist stopped and asked, "How far does the road go?" Mother answered, "All the way." Her answer proved to be prophetic: each of us got on that road and traveled all the way. We have looked back now and then, but never gone back to stay.

CHAPTER 13

Knowledge is Power;
Wisdom is Strength

THESE RAPER SIBLINGS stemmed from the strict structure of a loving family taught to care not only for each other but for the community as a whole. With that beginning, they learned to reap the harvest of a visionary father and supportive mother who taught them morality, the ways of hard work, and the means to achieve rewarding goals through learning and discovery. Theirs was part of a general movement from rural to urban America at a time when advanced education offered new and varied opportunities beyond farming. The movement sprang from two basic roots: leadership within the local community, and encouragement from a federal government willing to match communal efforts. Both forces worked together to use developing technology for building something new and different. The Raper experience personalizes a movement that perhaps could have happened only in a relatively new, expandable country such as the United States of America in the early part of the twentieth century.

On a personal level, who did all these Raper siblings grow up to be? How did each contribute to the world at large?

Starting with the youngest—the nugget of my desire to organize and present this dialogue of Rapers—**John** grew up to lead a somewhat troubled yet productive life. I met him during my senior year at the University of Chicago in 1946. He, a newly arrived Assistant Professor of Botany, became my mentor in science. As his first graduate student, I worked with him on the sex life of *Achlya*—that little water mold Kenneth mentioned—then, later, on a wood-rotting mushroom called *Schizophyllum* with 20,000 sexes. We spent the rest of our scientific lives together trying to figure out who could mate with whom and how.

John, being very red headed, preferred the name Red. While his siblings always called him John, I succumbed to his preference. Red not only taught me to love the fungi and the many quirks of their various life styles, he also taught me the meaning of love between man and woman. Alas, when we met, he was married. Nonetheless and shockingly, we fell in love and, after three traumatic years, resolved our dilemma in marriage to each other soon after his divorce.

I have never known such a man as Red Raper—driven, quixotic, brilliant, passionate, innovative, and, by today's terminology, somewhat bipolar—he could soar with high spirits, sustain energetic levels of productive activity, then crash with occasional fits of depression of no apparent cause. With all this, Red achieved worldwide eminence as a scientist, having been elected Fellow of the American Academy of Arts and Sciences, Fellow of the National Academy of Sciences, and Chair of Harvard's Department of Biology during which he died of a heart attack at the age of sixty-two. We had an exciting, somewhat fitful, yet fruitful life together.

Having listened to Red and his siblings talk about their formative years, I came to understand considerably more about how his values developed, the origin of his resentments, and why he became the man he was.

Kenneth achieved even greater fame. He not only received the honors of Fellowship in the American Academy of Arts and Sciences and The National Academy of Science, but the American Philosophical Society, and an honorary doctorate from the University of North Carolina as well.

Both Ken and John graduated from the University of North Carolina, Chapel Hill, and obtained Masters and Doctoral degrees in Botany at Harvard University. Ken's part in the discovery of a fungal strain capable of producing industrial quantities of penicillin during World War II attracted international attention at a critical time in world history.

Kenneth became a scholar and a gentleman, and, with wife Louise, not only engaged the best hotels while traveling, but hosted elegant gatherings in their home.

Blanche, the only female, grew to be a high school teacher of history and English in Winston-Salem, North Carolina, and went on to obtain a master's degree in history from Wake Forest University. Following Frank's example of serving the community, Blanche became an avid participant and leader in activist groups including the League of Women Voters, the Women's International League for Peace and Freedom, and the American Association of University Women. Having had enough of the Methodist and Moravian churches of her childhood, she switched commitment to the more liberal Unitarian-Universalist faith as an adult. As her parents had wished, Blanche married Aubrey Zimmerman, "the right sort of man," who grew up of good stock on a neighboring farm, achieved a college degree in finance, and became an accountant at Duke Power Company. A widow at seventy-six, intrepid Blanche moved to Santa Cruz, California, where she spent 18 years continuing her activist endeavors in new, exciting surroundings. She never stopped writing hymns and poetry and often performed in theatrical settings.

Howard attained the highest paid profession of the lot, having worked his way up in the banking business to presidency of the First Federal Building and Loan in Burlington, North Carolina. He stuck with Methodism becoming a trustee of the church and lead in many local activities including service as treasurer of the YMCA and president of the North Carolina Savings and Loan League. Howard's agility with numbers more than made up for his lack of facility for spelling. He and wife Catherine lived a comfortable life in a lovely, well-kept home, played golf and bridge at the Country Club, and entertained properly—the Southern way.

In his own words, Howard declares, "I didn't take to tobacco suckering any more than what John did. I mean, I'm a pretty good "coupling pole rider" when it comes to that, and I can ride that way when I have to; but 'less there's a need, I prefer a more comfortable seat. That's largely what I've got, I think, in the Savings and Loan business. Sure, I enjoy the income right much, but even more, I like the work with the people, and I like to help folks get the homes they want for themselves. 'Course there are times when we have to foreclose too, and I don't enjoy that part of it, but by and large it's a much better kind of life for me than what I would 'uv had on the farm all my life."

Ralph, with a bachelors degree in business administration and a masters in education, married Musette and ascended to the position of deputy director of the Cotton Division in the United States Department of Agriculture where he served for thirty years. He became a world leading expert on cotton commodities and received an award from the USDA for Superior Service.

Ralph was chided by his siblings as the only sibling who ever signed a million dollar check during his career.

Arthur achieved worldwide fame as author of several books on the problems of rural development in the South during the nineteen thirties: *Tenants of the Almighty, Sharecroppers All, The Tragedy of Lynching, Preface to Peasantry,* and *Rural Development in Action.* An early advocate of civil rights, he worked on various commissions addressing racial discrimination. Arthur resigned his faculty position at Agnes Scott College in Decatur, Georgia in 1939 after the college administration chastised him for taking his white students to visit the all black Tuskegee University as part of their education.

Arthur moved on to a career as social scientist and research analyst for several federal government agencies and, in the aftermath of World War II, served as advisor for United States' policies on rural development in Asia, North Africa, and the Middle East. In his final assignment as senior advisor to the Pakistan Academy for Rural Development, Arthur, with help from wife Martha, applied most successfully the lessons of communal self-help he had learned from his youth in Welcome, North Carolina. He worked with local leaders in what was then called East Pakistan to encourage the farmers themselves to take an interest in and be responsible for improved farming practices—a bottom-up rather than top-down approach.

Luther, after earning bachelors and masters degrees in agriculture from North Carolina State College, Raleigh, married Rachel, a spirited southern gal, and went on to develop a thirty-two year career promoting farmer-owned cooperatives. Starting as assistant director for distribution of goods, he became director of membership relations in Southern States Cooperative, the largest farmers' cooperative in the South. Luther was the first to establish and sell Zyosia grass for cultivation in Virginia.

Looking back, he comments, "That plot of Zyozia we keep growing and selling plugs out of (just for the fun of it) has started right many hearty lawns all over the Southeast. Generally speaking, though, a good bit more satisfaction came from my work with the cooper-

KNOWLEDGE IS POWER; WISDOM IS STRENGTH

atives—far more, I think, than would have been possible had I stayed put in Welcome these seventy some years. It has given me a special sense of worth, helping farmers pool their resources to help each other. I'm grateful for the contacts with all the people involved, and I'll have to confess, I've liked being in a position where my advice would be listened to occasionally.

'Course I think maybe we missed something, getting away from the demands of farm life and by and large the kinds of wholesome activities that went on in Welcome while we were growing up there—I mean in terms of how our children were brought up— maybe they don't appreciate their comforts and rewards so much as we of our generation did; things have come a mite easier for them than they have for us. But they're fine youngsters, not too spoiled, seem to be doing right well too, and we're proud of 'em, every last one."

Cletus, as mentioned in the dialogue presented here, grew up to have big dreams. He graduated with a major in finance from Guilford College, a North Carolinian Quaker institution, and, after serving in World War I, teamed up with a partner to make a version of the balloon tire for automobiles. Cletus aimed to become a millionaire by patenting this invention. Alas, he and his partner made the mistake of developing their invention in a space leased from one of the big tire companies. Despite monetary contributions from the Raper family for legal aid, the company out-lawyered them and won the patent for itself. Cletus, with wife Gertrude's loving help, recovered from defeat and succeeded in attaining a well-paid position as financial director for Murray-Hill Construction Company in Cleveland, Ohio—while dabbling in politics on the side.

Arthur adds a personal note:

"Now how has all this settled out? Well I won't, in fact I can't, speak for the rest of you, but I, as one, am grateful to have gotten away from the family farm. Now, in retirement, I'm glad to be back on my own little place, just for the pleasure of it.

But my life's work is in sociological studies: the close association with some very fine fellow workers in the field, such as Ralph Bunch, Lillian Smith, Gunnar Myrdal—just to mention a few whose names most folks would recognize—the working in many different countries where I had the opportunity of collaborating with other talented people in cultures wholly different from our own, and the satisfaction of feeling that I've made some contribution in efforts to understand, develop, and improve communities in many areas of the world. Some of these failed but not all.

These things have afforded me a richer, more challenging kind of existence than I believe would have been possible had I not left Welcome. Still, the growing up in Welcome came first and was important. I am proud to be a Raper, I am proud to have learned to work the land, I am proud to be a Southerner.

Speaking of pride in being a Raper, I have to add to my expounding here to tell you of an incident that happened to our eldest, Charlie, while he was serving as platoon leader during the Korean War:

One of his duties was to see to it that his dozen or so fellows were all lined up periodically for inspection, neat and at attention with their name tags on straight. On one such occasion Charles Raper was late. He just barely managed to get the men in order and unfold himself in line when the captain appeared.

The captain, a tough and gruff one, inspected each man carefully, and when he got to Charlie he looked especially critical. "Young man," he growled, "are you proud of your name?" Charlie, standing stiffly, staring straight ahead, deliberated for a time trying to make up his mind whether to haul off and bust him one, or take it on the chin. He strained finally to his full height and shouted back, 'Yes, sir!' whereupon the Captain said, in a somewhat softer tone, 'Well then, son, turn your name tag over so all of us can read it.'"

EPILOGUE

NOT ONLY the Raper clan but Welcome itself moved on. No longer a farming community, it has morphed into a budding suburb of Winston-Salem as announced by its current signpost of entry, "Welcome to Welcome: A Friendly Place," with displays of small town activities such as Lions Club, Boy Scouts, Garden Club, Fire Fighters.

The Raper homestead no longer exists, having been burned for practice by the local Fire Fighters Association. It has since been replaced by an electrically wired, modest brick house with attached garage, close by a well paved road.

Frank and Julia's children are all gone now. The boys seemed to have inherited their father's frail heart in varying degrees. John, the youngest, died the youngest at sixty-two. Luther, Arthur, and Howard made it to the age of eighty. Blanche outlived them all, dying of natural causes at the age of nearly ninety-four. Each sibling married and started another generation. In total they spawned sixteen children, all of whom succeeded in obtaining good productive livelihoods. As in the past, the Raper descendants and their families continue to gather every five years in honor of their heritage.

Welcome to modern-day Welcome.